Professional Issues in Work with Babies and Toddlers

Early childhood provision for babies and toddlers is in a critical phase. While governments are pushing for fast-paced expansion, mainly to support the return of mothers to the labour market, early childhood experts are deeply concerned about the quality of provision on offer for children up to age three. Research has consistently demonstrated that well-qualified educators are a crucial component towards ensuring a climate of sensitivity and responsiveness to individual children – and thus a central ingredient of high quality provision. However, national policy choices regarding required professional education/training and required resources for supporting the well-being and learning opportunities of very young children are highly variable.

The chapters in this book approach the topic of professional work with very young children in diverse ways, employing varying theoretical frameworks, research foci and research methodologies. They illustrate starkly divergent policy contexts, in this case predominantly European, with research located in Belgium, France, Finland, Italy, Sweden and the UK, but also in South Africa and the USA.

This book will be of interest to those conducting research into provision for infants and toddlers, both at the micro-level of relationships and settings and at the macro-level of policy paradigms. Potential readers also include practitioners and prospective managers and leaders of early childhood centres, as well as those offering initial and postgraduate early years teacher education and continuing professional development courses.

This book was originally published as a special issue of *Early Years*.

Pamela Oberhuemer is affiliated to the State Institute of Early Childhood Research in Munich, Germany. She was lead researcher of a government funded study on Systems of Early Years Education and Professional Training in Europe (SEEPRO), and of a six-country study on continuing professional learning systems commissioned by WiFF, a nation-wide early years workforce initiative in Germany. Pamela has acted as an early years consultant to the OECD (Starting Strong reviews) and UNESCO.

Liz Brooker is a Reader in Early Childhood at the Institute of Education in London, UK. She spent many years as an early years teacher before returning to research and teaching in the university, and her experience of working with young children and their families has informed her research and publications on ethnic minority children's learning at home and school, on transitions, on infants and toddlers, and most recently, on play.

Rod Parker-Rees is Coordinator of Early Childhood Studies at Plymouth University, UK, where he has developed and led programmes at undergraduate and masters' level. He has edited *Meeting the Child in Steiner Kindergartens: An Exploration of Beliefs, Values and Practices* and has co-edited *Early Years Education (Major Themes in Education)* and *Early Childhood Studies: An Introduction to the Study of Children's Worlds and Children's Lives*.

Professional Issues in Work with Babies and Toddlers

Edited by
Pamela Oberhuemer, Liz Brooker and Rod Parker-Rees

Routledge
Taylor & Francis Group

LONDON AND NEW YORK

First published 2014
by Routledge
2 Park Square, Milton Park, Abingdon, Oxon, OX14 4RN, UK

and by Routledge
711 Third Avenue, New York, NY 10017, USA

Routledge is an imprint of the Taylor & Francis Group, an informa business

British Library Cataloguing in Publication Data
A catalogue record for this book is available from the British Library

ISBN 13: 978-0-415-73492-9

Typeset in Times New Roman
by Taylor & Francis Books

Publisher's Note
The publisher accepts responsibility for any inconsistencies that may have arisen during the conversion of this book from journal articles to book chapters, namely the possible inclusion of journal terminology.

Disclaimer
Every effort has been made to contact copyright holders for their permission to reprint material in this book. The publishers would be grateful to hear from any copyright holder who is not here acknowledged and will undertake to rectify any errors or omissions in future editions of this book.

Contents

Citation Information

The chapters in this book were originally published in *Early Years*, volume 32, issue 2 (July 2012). When citing this material, please use the original page numbering for each article, as follows:

Chapter 6

Community-based learning to support South African early group care
Virginia Casper and Faith Lamb-Parker
Early Years, volume 32, issue 2 (July 2012) pp. 183–199

Chapter 7

Socio-spatial practices in a Finnish daycare group for one- to three-year-olds
Niina Rutanen
Early Years, volume 32, issue 2 (July 2012) pp. 201–214

Chapter 8

What counts when working with mathematics in a toddler-group?
Camilla Björklund
Early Years, volume 32, issue 2 (July 2012) pp. 215–228

Chapter 9

'Wasted down there': policy and practice with the under-threes
Rory McDowall Clark and Sue Baylis
Early Years, volume 32, issue 2 (July 2012) pp. 229–242

Please direct any queries you may have about the citations to
clsuk.permissions@cengage.com

Notes on Contributors

Jean-Marie Barbier, Centre de Recherche sur la Formation (CRF), Conservatoire des Arts et Métiers (CNAM), Paris, France

Sue Baylis, Institute of Education, University of Worcester, Worcester, UK

Camilla Björklund, Department of Education, Communication and Learning, Gothenburg University, Gothenburg, Sweden

Virginia Casper, Bank Street College of Education, New York City, USA and University of Johannesburg, Johannesburg, South Africa

Peter Elfer, Department of Education, Froebel College, University of Roehampton, London, UK

Donatella Giovannini, Department of Education, City of Pistoia, Italy

Kathy Goouch, Department of Professional Development, Canterbury Christ Church University, Canterbury, UK

Faith Lamb-Parker, Bank Street College of Education, New York City, New York, USA

Susanna Mayer, Institute of Cognitive Sciences and Technologies, National Research Council of Italy, Rome, Italy

Rory McDowall Clark, Institute of Education, University of Worcester, Worcester, UK

Tullia Musatti, Institute of Cognitive Sciences and Technologies, National Research Council of Italy, Rome, Italy

Mariacristina Picchio, Institute of Cognitive Sciences and Technologies, National Research Council of Italy, Rome, Italy

Florence Pirard, Department of Education and Training, University of Liège, Liège, Belgium

Sacha Powell, Research Centre for Children, Families and Communities, Canterbury Christ Church University, Canterbury, UK

Susan L. Recchia, Curriculum and Teaching, Teachers College, Columbia University, New York, USA

Niina Rutanen, School of Education/Early Childhood Education, University of Tampere, Tampere, Finland

Introduction

This issue of *Early Years* is a 'special issue'. It focuses exclusively on research relating to professional care and education work with children up to the age of three. It is also a 'bumper issue'. Instead of the usual six or seven papers, this one includes nine, reflecting the encouraging response to the editors' Call for Papers.

The papers are predominantly European, with authors located in the French Community of Belgium, France, Finland, Italy, Sweden and the UK (England), but also in South Africa and the USA, thus providing some indication of the growing international spread of journal writers and readers. For example, the 'top twenty' countries downloading *Early Years* articles in 2011 included nine European, four Asian, two North American, two Australasian, two African countries and one Middle Eastern country. During the same year, papers were submitted from 19 countries, ranging from Croatia, Egypt and India to Iran and the Sultanate of Oman, and accepted from 17 countries, including China, Jordan and the United Arab Emirates.

This issue's papers approach the topic of professional work with very young children in diverse ways, employing varying theoretical frameworks, research foci and research methodologies. The reports also illustrate the starkly divergent policy contexts in which this research takes place.

We start with two papers which draw on the narratives of early childhood practitioners. The first one takes us into 25 'baby rooms' located in early childhood centres in England. In these rooms, designated 'key persons' work with children up to 18 months of age. The compelling title, 'Whose hand rocks the cradle?', hints at the competing discourses – public and private, explicit and implicit – which surround this work. Sacha Powell and Kathy Goouch explore the tensions between these discourses as seen by the key persons participating in the study. They draw on a variety of sources – individual interviews, facilitated focus-group discussions and unsolicited discussions on the project's online social networking site. A key research question was: Whose judgement counts most in everyday practices? The practitioners' ways of dealing with prevailing discourses appear to oscillate between accepting the behaviours demanded by 'privileged voices' (e.g. official guidance), while simultaneously expressing resistance and feeling undervalued. The authors conclude that on the one hand there is a danger that narrowly conceptualised regulatory practices may disempower practitioners; on the other hand they suggest that caregivers may also 'collude in their own oppression'. Providing space for facilitated collegial dialogue is seen as a much-needed and valuable vehicle both for heightening awareness of performativity expectations and for developing a critical and challenging professional stance towards dominant discourses.

Critical professional reflection among colleagues is also at the heart of Peter Elfer's paper. Nine nursery managers, again in England, were given the opportunity to talk about the emotional demands of their work. In two-hour Work Discussions (WD) (a concept emanating from psychoanalytic theory), which were held monthly over a period of 10 months, the participants were encouraged, together with a group facilitator, to reflect on the emotional challenges of their work with children. However, topics chosen for discussion focused almost exclusively on the managers' own emotional issues, including the perceived over-dependence of staff on manager guidance, the preoccupation of staff in the workplace with personal issues, repeated absenteeism and breaches of procedures. Using a grounded theory approach, the WD sessions were recorded, transcribed and coded, with back-up data coming from interviews and monthly diaries. The paper concludes with some open questions about controlling the agenda of Work Discussions, what can reasonably be expected of the procedure as a form of critical reflection on practice, and the role of group facilitators.

The research reported by Susan Recchia is part of a larger study aiming to explore multiple aspects of continuity in child care. The focus in this paper is on the relationship-building process between children and their caregivers. Using a variety of research procedures (assessment instruments detailing attachment and child–caregiver relationships, developmental reports, student caregiver journals and caregiver interviews), two boys aged two and a half attending a university campus child care centre in the USA are followed in their transition from the infant/toddler room to the preschool room. Although both had had positive relationships with their key caregivers in the infant room, the transition to a larger group without a specific 'key person' turned out to be more challenging for one than the other. It is suggested that both the sending caregivers (by helping children to anticipate the changes the transition may bring) and the new caregiving adults (by giving them time to ease themselves into the new environment) can support transitions in ways that foster secure relationships. A key insight from the study is that 'Relationship building is a dynamic process which requires time, patience, flexibility and commitment'.

The two papers that follow focus on innovative practices in Italy and in the French-speaking community of Belgium and France. Both relate to new approaches towards the continuing professional development of practitioners working in infant/toddler centres. Mariacristina Picchio, Donatella Giovannini, Susanna Mayer and Tullia Musatti, all established researchers in the Italian context of provision for under-threes, report on a series of action research projects in the municipality of Pistoia. Five researchers collaborated with pedagogic coordinators and practitioners over a period of three years, aiming to enhance collegial discourse around the topic of systematic documentation and analysis of the children's experiences. The procedure of writing (weekly reports, process reports), although not initially welcomed by some, turned out to be a powerful tool for sustaining memories of individual and shared reflective processes, and for tracking the pathways of individual children over time. The research showed that if realistic documentary practices can be found and agreed upon and if reflection-in-action becomes a regular part of collegial activity, even the difficult task of composing process reports (retrospective accounts of learning processes requiring a high level of abstraction and reflection-on-action) can be made less onerous if collegial support is available.

Florence Pirard from Belgium and Jean-Marie Barbier from France present the concept of 'accompaniment' as a supportive and transformative approach towards developing professional competences on the job. 'Accompaniment' is a familiar term in training contexts in the French-speaking countries, seen as an ongoing, interactive and open process between a resource person and a practitioner. Linked to a wider theoretical framework of education and training cultures, a 'culture of professionalisation' presupposes that both actors and action can be mutually and simultaneously transformed through a process of co-construction based on shared observation, discussion and argumentation. The initial case study research took place in the French Community of Belgium, where practitioners in infant/toddler centres tend to have considerably lower formal levels of qualification than those working with three- to six-year-olds. Following the introduction of new curricular guidelines, the 'accompaniment' process focused in particular on supporting the self-regulating and participatory evaluation of everyday practices. The aim was to help practitioners develop shared criteria rather than implement external standards, and to support them in reflecting on the complexities of practice and in constructing new knowledge together with colleagues, parents and children.

The next paper is also about a co-constructive and participatory approach towards curriculum development, but in a very different context, and with very different overall societal goals. Virginia Casper and Faith Lamb-Parker report on their action research work in four of the nine provinces in South Africa. The Developing Families Project-SA is set within the wider framework of an integrative approach towards HIV/AIDS prevention and aims to foster learning among family and community members regarding the support, care and education of very young, vulnerable children. Over a five-year period, and within a small-group, community-based learning approach, involving parents and stakeholders from local early childhood, health and NGO organisations, the researchers were able to open opportunities for 'candid discussions' about child-rearing and women's roles which would not have been possible within a formalised teaching/training setting. From their accumulated observations, interviews and focus-group discussions over time, the authors conclude that work with the youngest children in South Africa is very much 'work in progress'. Community caregivers – often women living in poverty – may feel tempted to accept ever increasing numbers of children into their care facilities. In some cases this can lead to a situation where up to 50 young children are placed with only one adult in a single room. The authors emphasise in conclusion that strong advocacy efforts are needed to stimulate public debate and policy initiatives which scrutinise the seriously conflicting economic needs of entrepreneurial caregivers and emotional needs of very young children.

The provision predicament in South Africa contrasts starkly with the privileged situation of children and families in Europe, particularly in the Nordic countries, where well-resourced early childhood centres, including rooms for infants and toddlers, have been firmly established for decades. Niina Rutanen presents research in one such setting in Finland. Drawing on a theoretical framework influenced by critical geography and the work of Henri Lefebvre, and using ethnographic observations and video-elicited discussions and interviews with three practitioners, the qualitative case study examines everyday practices from a socio-spatial perspective. Space is understood as 'conceived space', 'perceived space' and 'lived space', and the author focuses on perceived space, i.e. on the appropriation of space in early childhood settings in an empirically observable and visible way. According to three categories constructed from the ethnographic data – areas with a predefined objective and location (e.g. mealtimes, sleeping); transition areas (e.g. dressing for outdoor play); and areas with flexible objectives and locations (e.g. outdoor play space) – she analysed how the rules for these areas were adapted or reassigned according to the age of the children. The author suggests that initial and continuing professional development activities should pay more attention to a critical analysis of socio-spatial practices, thereby enhancing understandings of possibly ingrained institutional structures in early childhood settings.

Another paper by a Finnish researcher (currently based in Sweden) looks at toddlers' explorations of mathematical concepts within both self-initiated play and planned activities. Camilla Björklund draws on 'Variation Theory' and the concept of 'Learning Studies' to illustrate how educators can develop strategies for supporting mathematics learning even with very young children. Videographic data are used for analysing educator–child interactions, complemented by a meta-analysis for self-evaluation purposes and an interview with the educator. Being able to spot opportunities for exploring mathematical phenomena in everyday activities, strengthening the children's awareness of similarities and differences, introducing nuanced ways of describing variations in size, and using the children's interests as a starting point were considered to be the key professional competences for supporting mathematical learning.

We conclude this special issue with a third paper from England. After outlining recent legislation and curricular frameworks that emphasise a holistic approach towards the education and care of children up to school age, Rory McDowall Clark and Sue Baylis argue that when it comes to babies and toddlers a rhetorical gap still persists between policy statements and contemporary practices. Bridging this gap requires new approaches to practitioner preparation. In order to qualify for Early Years Professional Status (EYPS), a recently introduced award to boost the low number of graduate-led settings, candidates are required to spend time with babies and toddlers. Lave and Wenger's learning community approach provides the theoretical framework for the researchers' interactions with EYP candidates – in this case all experienced practitioners working across the sector in state-maintained nursery schools, private nurseries, pre-schools (playgroups) and children's centres. They observe how the EYP candidates were stimulated to rethink their professional values and working practices through their explorations of work with babies and toddlers.

This collection of papers illustrates just some of the considerable challenges facing researchers who choose to focus on professional work with children in their earliest years. A variety of sensitive research procedures is needed to ensure that the perspectives of very young children, who have their own energetic modes of expression, and the perspectives of practitioners, who may not have been supported in initial or continuing professional development to express their views confidently, are reported in an ethically responsible way.

Pamela Oberhuemer

Whose hand rocks the cradle? Parallel discourses in the baby room

Sacha Powell[a] and Kathy Goouch[b]

[a]Research Centre for Children, Families and Communities, Canterbury Christ Church University, Canterbury, UK; [b]Department of Professional Development, Canterbury Christ Church University, Canterbury, UK

This article explores the practice narratives of a group of 25 caregivers who work with babies in daycare settings in England and seeks to illustrate awareness of, resistance to and compliance with powerful discourses. It is argued that multiple voices exert an influence over baby room practice, disempowering the caregivers and reducing their capacity to practise in ways that meet the 'babies' best interests'. Yet there may also be ways in which they collude in their own oppression. Opportunities to engage in professional dialogue, reflection and critique as a means of *conscientização* (conscientization or 'dialogic cultural action' as described by Freire in *Pedagogy of the Oppressed* [London: Penguin, 1970], 141) are rare. When offered, these may simultaneously increase participants' awareness of discourses of performativity and inadequacy and heighten feelings of powerlessness, but may also offer a space in which to nourish professional knowledge and understanding and the self-confidence to challenge and resist privileged voices that sustain a hegemony.

Introduction

Daycare for babies and young children is big business with much of the world's daycare provision based in the private sector (Alderman and Vegas 2011). In England, many babies under 18 months of age spend time in formal (group) daycare settings, usually in dedicated 'baby rooms' with a key person designated as their primary caregiver (Powell and Goouch 2011). The cost of this service is normally borne by the baby's parent(s). The provision is governed by a national, statutory framework of learning, development and welfare requirements (DCSF 2008) which continues in a new, revised form (DfE 2012) and is assessed by a national inspection body, 'Ofsted'. Local authorities offer advisory services and training, and an array of statutory and voluntary agencies may also provide an input. The system allows for a multitude of voices to declare an interest in what constitutes appropriate/good/best/high-quality care for each baby. The plurality of perspectives opens up possibilities for contradiction, complexity, uncertainty and confusion. In the midst of this mêlée are the babies and the people who work in the baby rooms.

With evidence gathered from 25 English baby rooms, this paper explores the ways that the babies' most intimate caregivers in daycare settings described 'who controls the field of judgement' (Ball 2003, 216) in baby rooms, thereby shaping the babies' experiences of daycare.

A multitude of voices

The politics and practice of early childhood education and care (ECEC) are fraught with tensions and the issues become even more emotive when concerned with infants who may be little more than a few weeks old. The question of who is 'best' placed to care for babies and very young children has been informed, shaped and rationalised by evidence from different disciplines and research perspectives (Baldock, Fitzgerald, and Kay 2009). For many years, findings from developmental psychology, particularly studies concerned with attachment theories (e.g. Bowlby 1988; Ainsworth 1979; Schore 2001), generated heated debates about whether or not non-maternal care is detrimental in the short and longer term. The influence of these academic debates can be traced to public attitudes, social structures and policies for childcare provision (Belsky 2009).

Attempts to shift responsibilities for childcare away from the maternal domain have been based on feminist, economic and social inclusion/welfare arguments. During the 1970s feminist theorists began to draw attention to sexual discrimination in relation to socially constructed maternal identities and roles. Marxist feminists argued that childcare should be a responsibility of society in order to elevate women's social status (Humm 1995). More than 20 years after Barrett (1980) challenged state ideology in this respect, Manning-Morton (2006, 45) observed that childcare, an innately emotional occupation, has been de-professionalised because in a 'Cartesian world-view, caring for children from birth to three – a job that entails daily immersion in the physical frailty of bodily processes and in the intensity of unpredictable and fluctuating emotions – has been seen as an extension of women's "natural" domestic sphere'. Similar objections have been raised by Moss (2006), Ailwood (2008) and Osgood (2012) and suggest the persistence of hegemonic discourses that serve to devalue childcare as an occupation for women or men. Furthermore, it is argued that these discourses perpetuate circumstances in which we 'compensate our child care and preschool professionals at the level of unskilled parking lot attendants and taxi drivers' (Lash and McMullen 2008). This links to another sociopolitical issue: namely, the cost of childcare and ultimately who should pay for it.

Predominantly, parents in England foot the bill for their babies' formal childcare, much of which is based in the private sector following a rapid marketisation of provision encouraged by the former New Labour government (Penn 2008). Daycare providers are located within the state-maintained, private and independent/voluntary sectors but a charge to parents for childcare is levied across all sectors of provision. An annual survey of childcare provision in England revealed that around 57% of working families in England with a child under one year of age had used at least one form of (out-of-home) childcare in 2009 and this increased to 70% when the child was aged 1–2 years (Smith et al. 2010). Exploring maternity and paternity rights, Chanfreau et al. (2011) found that 55% of mothers who were employed prior to childbirth took no more than 39 weeks' maternity leave in 2008 and 51% were using some formal childcare when they returned to work. But the percentages of mothers who used only formal childcare for their babies increased in line with hourly income (19% using, earning less than £5 per hour; 46% using, earning more than £20 per hour). These parents face some of the highest childcare costs in the world, with an average expenditure of £97 per week for 25 hours of childcare for a child under two years of age (Save the Children and the Daycare Trust 2011).

Increased state investment and private expenditure on early childhood education and care (ECEC) and the availability and use of daycare places for babies have produced a myriad of 'stakeholders' whose interests may be 'compatible' or 'conflicting' (Figger and Schaltegger 2000, 9). Despite recent government policy documentation that promulgates harmonious 'co-production' among stakeholders (DfE 2011), many scholars have highlighted conflicts in their studies of conceptual, structural or pedagogic matters in ECEC (e.g. Moyles 2001; Colley 2006; Manning-Morton 2006; Elfer 2007; Lash and McMullen 2008; Brooker 2010; Kaga, Bennett, and Moss 2010; Powell 2010; Lee and Brotheridge 2011; Kroger 2011; Osgood 2012). Our own interest lies in whether it is possible for baby room caregivers to assert their own perspectives, to manipulate conflict to positive effect and to fulfil their stated, principal aim of 'serving the babies' best interests'?

Collecting baby room stories

In September 2009, a group of caregivers from 10 daycare settings in south-east England joined the Baby Room Project and in January 2011 the group extended to involve 25 settings. All but two of these were privately owned and all complied with the Government's requirement to be registered with the Office for Standards in Education, Children's Services and Skills (Ofsted) as a provider of ECEC under the guidance of the statutory *Early Years Foundation Stage* (EYFS) (DCSF 2008; DfE 2012) framework for the learning and development of children from birth to five. The 25 women ranged in age from 18 to 60 years with most being between 18 and 25 years old. They worked in baby rooms of different shapes and sizes, some with numerous colleagues, others with one or even none and in total 370 babies spent time in their baby rooms each week. Each had responsibility as key person for at least three babies with the maximum being eight over the course of a week. All held a relevant early years or childcare qualification but none was educated to degree level or above. Although many (but not all) reported that they had accessed some in-service training or professional development during the previous couple of years, for most this training related to practical health and safety issues, food safety, child protection or safeguarding. Many worked very long hours with infrequent, short breaks and some worked in near or total isolation from colleagues caring for older children. In one case, a participant reported spending many hours alone in her baby room with occasional 'glances' from her manager. The opportunities for professional dialogue were rare and they relished the chance to engage with other caregivers during the project's 'development sessions'.

The project's design comprised a hybrid of research and development activities and sources of evidence, which came from:

- semi-structured interviews with participants and their managers;
- video-recorded, naturalistic observations of the participants' work in their baby rooms;

- interviews with the parents of a sample of babies for whom the participants were the designated key person;
- facilitated group discussions based on extracts from policy texts, media reports, videos or research findings; and
- unsolicited discussions on the project's online social networking site (the Baby Room 'NING').

The evidence that forms the basis for this article is drawn from interviews with participants, and discussions in the development sessions and on the NING. Participants were involved on a voluntary basis and were repeatedly reminded of the project's aims: to explore what happens in baby rooms and to support the development of good practice and mutually supportive professional networks. We were acutely conscious of the complicated ethics surrounding their involvement in a combined research and development project and so we regularly explained our plans, discussed our tentative findings, and sought consent to involve them in different activities, to use their contributions as evidence at different stages during the project and to publish our findings.

Although each participant brought different stories, many had similar experiences to share and from within these stories emerged a theme of agency linked to self-perception, occupational status and the perceived governance, regulation or surveillance of their practice. The examples we have used in this article were brought to us by individual caregivers and reflect the specific context in which each worked. But the general themes that each one illustrates, which we have identified as concerning power and agency, typified the situation of most or all of the participants. Where there was disagreement, this has been highlighted.

We did not actively seek to discuss power, agency and resistance (or compliance) with our participants in the Baby Room Project; these subjects emerged through the course of discussions. Rather than asking direct questions about power, we continued to collect stories and set about analysing these in ways we believed could expose this power and agency. But building on others' work on this subject, our analytical framework was deductive, seeking evidence in response to two key questions: 'Who controls the field of judgement?' (power), and 'How do participants react?' (compliance/resistance). But we also explored how the participants' responses served to sanction and sustain or to oppose and change the situation as they described it. This follows Stones's (2005, 81) critique and redevelopment of Giddens's (1984) Structuration Theory in which he proposes that, 'The duality of structure and agency within the agent…is central both to structure as the medium of practices, and to the production of structure as the outcome of practice'. Our exploration was concerned with resistance to hegemonic discourses or the *re*-production of [powerful] structures. We explored each through the participants' narratives and found evidence of 'naive compliance' (Freire 1970) and 'passive resistance' (Osgood 2006a); but little evidence of 'strategic compliance' (Lacey 1977) characterised by practice as 'a technical act rather than a personal activity' (Goouch 2008, 93).

Spheres of influence

As argued earlier, we suggest that there exists a wide range of possible influences on how ECEC practice evolves and how baby room caregivers see themselves. The

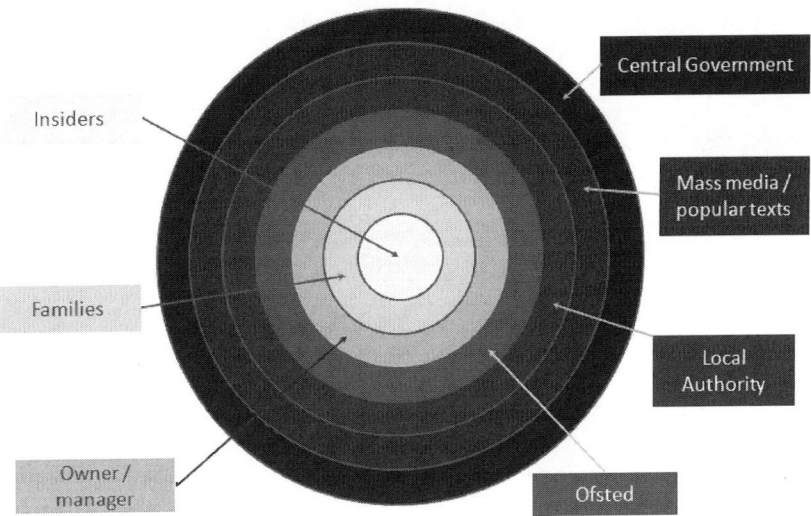

Figure 1. Seven Significant Spheres.

participants in our project expressed their own ideas about who or what shaped their practice and had greatest proximity or influence over their work. Working in small groups and then together, they developed a model, which we have called, 'Seven Significant Spheres' (see Figure 1) intended to highlight the sources of information and influence they perceived to be important. They placed themselves at the centre, along with baby room colleagues, as 'insiders'.

As we show later, the perceived distribution of power across these spheres varied and the participants told us different stories but these shared a common theme of coercion and control, which is explored in this article. In the next section, we illustrate each of the different spheres of influence with a story that exemplifies this theme.

From within the field of judgement

Insiders: it's child protection

In the initial interviews with practitioners, during development day discussions and in a task in which they were invited to draw and comment on the rooms in which they worked, the practitioners reported that 'child protection' was a significant influence on the physical environment in which they worked and the ways in which they operated within the baby rooms. In particular, those whose rooms afforded a separate, enclosed space for nappy changing and/or sleeping reported that working CCTV cameras or audio 'listening' devices had been installed. Initial comments as to the purposes of the equipment were, 'It's health and safety, isn't it' or 'for child protection'. However, when probed, the practitioners' statements that the CCTV cameras needed to be there in case any parents made allegations against a practitioner revealed that the primary purpose appeared not to be the protection of the children, but the protection of the practitioners themselves as they lived with the fear of (unfounded) child abuse allegations. The cameras were deemed to be a necessity, although they were also seen as a source of invasion of privacy for the babies as they slept or had their nappies changed.

Parents/manager: 'it's child abuse to keep them awake'

The issue of responding to parents' desires was mentioned earlier in relation to intimacy with the babies. The complexity of balancing parental wishes and 'needs' with other policies and practices or practitioners' beliefs also emerged in a discussion of babies' sleep routines. Several of the practitioners acknowledged the difficulties they faced when parents asked them not to allow a baby to go to sleep during a session at the setting. Comments included, 'We've been told [by manager and LA adviser] that it's child abuse to keep them awake when they need to sleep' and 'What can you do? Parents blame you if they [babies] wake up in the night because they have had a sleep at nursery.' And 'all the guidance is saying different things'. The practitioners unanimously agreed that babies should be allowed to sleep if they needed to, but said that this was not always possible because a parent had given strict instructions that a baby should not have a nap at nursery. They wanted to act in the 'babies' best interests' and therefore saw their professional knowledge quashed in favour of 'pleasing the parents' or, in a minority of cases, were overruled by a manager who, for example, it was said 'sits in an office doing policy and doesn't know the babies at all'.

Manager/parents: 'we're not allowed to kiss the babies'

During a lively discussion in a development day session, the practitioners talked about the importance of love, and explained how their days included time for them to 'cuddle the babies', which they enjoyed. However, one practitioner reported that it was a policy in her setting that she and her colleagues were 'not allowed to kiss the babies'. As the discussion ensued, she reported that this policy had been implemented by the setting's manager because 'parents don't want us to get too close to the babies'. She added that one mother had expressed her unease about physical closeness and so a blanket policy of 'no kissing' had been introduced by the setting's manager and this then applied to all the babies and children. Other participants reacted with shock and concern but confessed they too felt nervous about 'getting too close to the babies' for fear of upsetting a parent.

Ofsted: 'so that the babies can choose'

When asked in a development day session how they responded to the EYFS requirements to provide opportunities for babies to choose and lead different activities, the practitioners discussed their practice of putting out nearly all or all of the available toys and resources at any given time. When asked why they did this, comments included, 'because Ofsted says we have to' and 'so that the babies can choose'. Their comments revealed a common thread that ran through many of the discussions, which was the sense that rules were imposed on them by external bodies and they reported that they responded to them unquestioningly. In fact, no such Ofsted 'rule' exists stating that all resources must be put out at once so that babies can choose from them. Furthermore, although the practitioners stated that this was their practice, the observation evidence showed that they did in fact bring out different resources at different times (e.g. musical instruments, books, dolls, crayons and paper), sometimes in adult-led activities and sometimes in response to a baby's indication that (s)he wanted a particular item. This suggested a tension that they felt between what they did, what they felt they should be doing (and publicly reported doing) and the apparently unrecognised mismatch between the two.

Local authority: 'it's well-being and involvement'

All the practitioners brought their settings' documentation for recording development to a development day session and swapped and discussed these. In one setting it was reported that the local authority had given them a recording sheet that had to be used. This included tick-box responses to particular questions:

- Rate the child's well-being (during the observed activity) on a scale of 1–5.
- What learning style has the child demonstrated during the activity? (Visual, auditory, kinaesthetic).
- A further question asking practitioners to 'identify the child's current schema'.

Although some of the practitioners recognised a link between the first question and 'Ferre Laevers' or said, 'It's well-being and involvement', they were unable to go into details about what this meant (see Laevers 1998; Laevers 2005) and had little knowledge or understanding of the 'schemas' to which reference was made (e.g. Athey 1990).

Government: observations and the EYFS

The practitioners in the group were eager to learn about the others' practices and, in particular, the approaches used for observing, recording and reporting the babies' development. Although they all were required to comply with the EYFS, which provides guidance for documenting young children's learning and development, the ways that each setting approached this varied. In some cases, observations were comparatively infrequent whereas in others they took place in a very regular and structured routine (twice daily in one setting). Similarly, providing information to families about the babies' learning and development differed from photos and notes written in a contact book that parents received each time their child had attended the setting, to more infrequent and ad hoc sharing of the information.

All the practitioners knew that the EYFS sets out specific areas of learning and development. However, they felt unsure about what these meant in practice and were not always confident about ascribing an observation to one or more of these areas for the purposes of recording development. One participant reflected that:

> ... there is a vast amount of paperwork involved, however it has now become a part of everyday work. As well as doing weekly planning the staff also do 'Learning Journeys'. These represent the children's development as they progress through the nursery, they are made up of observations, photos, some samples of work and parent input. They are then linked to the EYFS. We also do Individual Play Plans, roughly one per term. From knowing the point at which the child is progressing the IPP allows

us to pinpoint the next steps under the EYFS that the child can achieve, not what we feel they should be achieving.

Another argued that, 'It was easier when we did *Birth to Three Matters*', and 'If a parent asked me to explain how a photo or observation showed an area of learning or development, I wouldn't know what to say; I don't understand it'. Nevertheless, all the participants agreed that they spent many hours recording observations and maintaining documents about what the babies were doing each week.

General public/media: 'lowest of the low'

In one development session the participants were asked to consider their professional identities. We asked them, 'Who do you think you are?' and their responses were broadly similar to those found by Osgood (2010), highlighting the caring aspects of their roles. As the group reflected on one another's constructs of a professional identity, one notably proclaimed, 'In education, early years is at the bottom, isn't it? And in early years, we're the lowest of the low aren't we....' This view was not contradicted by her peers but greeted by a silent, nodding affirmation.

Perpetuating privileged views

The participants' stories revealed complex power tussles in which they were positioned, sometimes mindful, but on occasions seemingly oblivious to others' privileged views. Table 1 summarises our analysis of the examples provided in the previous section.

The participants repeatedly told us that they saw their primary function as to identify and respond to the babies' 'needs' but felt that they met with frequent obstacles to fulfilling this purpose in ways they felt were 'best'. In the first three examples cited earlier, the objections they shared with us to imposed 'rules' stemmed from a belief that these prevented them from serving 'babies' best inter-

Table 1. Summary of analysis.

Story	Who controls the field of judgement?	Participants' response	Structure sustained/changed?
1. It's child protection	Selves/colleagues	Passive resistant	Sustained
2. It's child abuse to keep them awake	Parents	Passive resistant	Sustained
3. We're not allowed to kiss the babies	Manager	Passive resistant	Sustained
4. So babies can choose	'Ofsted', selves	Naive compliant	Sustained
5. It's well-being and involvement	'Local Authority'	Naive compliant	Sustained
6. Observations and the EYFS	Government	Naive compliant	Sustained
7. Lowest of the low	General public, media	Passive resistant	Sustained

ests'. Consequently, although they consciously complied with others' demands, they did so begrudgingly and simultaneously felt that this compromised not only the babies' well-being but also their own intuitive judgement. These examples conform to Osgood's concept of passive resistance, which she says resonates with Foucault's ideas of 'bodies that are docile and capable' (2006b, 189).

In examples 4 to 6, the participants' stories suggested a practice of 'docile' compliance. But these were also typified by a seeming lack of awareness of how their actions conformed to structure as the 'medium of practice' and in so doing sustained the re-'production of structure as the outcome of practice'. This appeared to be an unconscious submission to the structures and their perpetuation of its regulation of their practice through this subordination. Such compliance might be explained by the view expressed in example 7 of their comparatively low status and their recognition of the 'discourses of inadequacy' (Goouch and Powell forthcoming) that are frequently disseminated through the media and which Sachs (2003, 5) argues, 'have become powerful in setting education agendas'. Freire (1970) refers to this apparent lack of awareness not as unconsciousness but as 'naive consciousness', which contributes to the internalisation of oppressive structures, rules or discourses and thereby to collusion in one's own oppression.

The participants' own voices were seldom, if ever, heard within the cacophony that had come to characterise their baby room rules of practice. They told us of their dissatisfaction with imposed policies and procedures that they saw as inappropriate, irrelevant or unhelpful. These were agendas of which they were conscious and pertained to the spheres of influence positioned most closely to themselves, with the exception of the media. But they rarely challenged these in the setting (although were beginning to do so towards the end of the project).

However, their compliance with the rules imposed by more distal influences did not appear to be a conscious attempt to conform to a particular mode of practice that would constitute attempting, 'to satisfy the demands for performativity and technicist practice' (Osgood 2006a, 5). This was not because they did not feel the regulatory gaze that characterises such practice – and indeed their stories were rife with examples of surveillance, not least the recent introduction of CCTV cameras covering all areas of some baby rooms – but because they had had insufficient opportunities to understand *how* to perform and hence to consider whether or not to comply or resist.

In contrast, any evidence of 'performativity' suggested collusion with an internalised construct of disempowerment (lowest of the low). The low occupational status of the early years is widely perceived by those within the sector and well documented (Hargreaves and Hopper 2006). Indeed, the Nutbrown Review of Early Years and Childcare Qualifications (Nutbrown 2012) sought ideas on how to improve the public's perception of early years work. But as Moyles (2001) noted, the caring qualities of early years practitioners (such as upholding the babies' privacy) can diminish their value as professionals amongst those outside the sector and they may lack the strength to promote their views. In some respects, the baby room participants appeared similarly diminished and controlled in their practice despite voicing resistance in the project group. Recchia and Shin (2010) have highlighted the emotional investment and tensions that arise in caring for very young children, and it is precisely the emotionality of the profession which Colley (2006, 2) says makes practitioners particularly susceptible to 'prescription and control by dominant groups'. Field (2008) sees the ability to deploy strategies to cope with emotional complexities as a form of agency. The Baby Room Project participants' coping strategies appeared to oscillate between acceptance of regulated behaviour with an underlying confidence in their own judgement and sense of being undervalued and overlooked; and participation in and perpetuation of dominant or oppressive discourses. Freire makes a distinction between naive consciousness and intentionality in collusion with oppression. Adams, Bell, and Griffin (2007, 45) describe the latter as the means through which the oppressed may 'live to fight another day'.

Parallel discourses of oppression and resistance

Osgood (2006b, 189) argues that powerlessness may stem from practitioners not having, 'sufficient belief in themselves as "professionals" to challenge top-down policy implementation'. Yet the stories told by the Baby Room Project participants did not position these caregivers as wholly passive and compliant with dominant demands and discourses, nor did they present direct and overt challenges. From our perspective as participant observers, there appeared to be two simultaneous narratives coexisting:

- Awareness of the 'rules of practice' imposed by others, intentionality in collusion through passive resistance: awareness of being deemed by others as 'lowest of the low', resisting such discourses through assertions of the importance of their own intuitive judgements but complying through their actions with the demands of others whose voices were privileged, as in the sleeping example.
- Naive consciousness of dominant discourses, such as the 'Ofsted rule' about toys, and unintentional collusion through internalisation of dominant discourses and compliance (even misguided compliance as in the case of putting out all the toys) with (perceived) demands that would nevertheless fall short of strategic compliance.

Ball argues (2006, 47) that, 'Policies typically posit a restructuring, redistribution and disruption of power relations so that different people can and cannot make claims to be able to do different things'. Although it may appear that the 'policies' described earlier disable the participants and render them powerless 'to do different things', it seems that neither an entirely conformist nor a resistant stance was assumed by these caregivers as a whole. A complex mixture of compliant and passive resistant narratives was found. In part, this is reminiscent of Francis's (2001, 166) ideas that, 'the self incorporates both contradiction and consistency; is constructed by the self and by others; and has agency but is also determined by discursive material forces. This account is flexible, able to incorporate the contradictory and complex nature of human interaction and power relations' (cited in Osgood 2006a, 10). This flexibility was demonstrated in some of the caregivers' responses to demands on their practice, determined and shaped by dominant discursive forces. These caregivers' partially resistant philosophy appeared based on their strong beliefs in their own experiential knowledge of the babies' needs and best interests within the domain of the baby rooms.

The participants often described their isolation from the rest of the setting, and their difference from other early years practitioners. This isolation seemed partly the result of structural factors including increased policy attention on older children (aged three and above) and those working with them; and partly self-imposed separation on the basis that work with babies required something quite different and specialised. The caregivers' lack of knowledge and understanding of policy and research was unsurprising given this isolation and a deficiency in training and professional development opportunities (Goouch and S. Powell. 2010). This disconnection with others was also a disconnection from technicist jargon or models of performativity and meant that their stories were therefore neither consciously reactionary nor complicit, but ran in parallel to such extraneous discourses.

Dominant, structural factors concerned with gender, class, the value of care/caring, consumerism, state intervention and regulation rendered them relatively disempowered and superficially compliant in the actions that sustained their subjugation. But notions of oppression and resistance only surfaced for the caregivers when they too looked in on their own practice (and that of others in the group), as though positioned as external observers. Peters and Lankshear (1994, 179) reflect on Freire's theory that, 'human becoming presupposes critical consciousness and liberation from constraints which prevent people from speaking their word'; they argue that, 'human becoming must be a process in which all people have an equal right to their voice ... in speaking of dialogue as the process in which humans become, Freire is drawing attention to the importance of equal, active participation in naming the world: in making and remaking reality through transforming action-reflection'.

How things might be different

When they were provided with opportunities to reflect on, discuss and critique the status quo, the Baby Room Project participants became more vociferous and confident. Managers began to report that they saw increasing strength of conviction as well as critical reflection and dialogue within the baby rooms and, where possible, their settings more generally. Importantly, this was also being translated into action (Durrant 2010).

Gleeson and Knights (2006, 278) have argued that a reconciliation of agency and structure binaries will not produce lasting effects but leave, 'space for continuing debate and discourse around the tensions, conflicts and struggles through which creative transformations in professional practice might result.' They add that rather than research developing stereotypes of professional compliance, professionalism should be 'constructed through struggle from *within* the cracks, crevices and contradictions of practice' (original emphasis, ibid., 289). Stronach et al. (2002) are cynical regarding 'narratives of professional redemption' in which 'the professional must be rescued from the iron cage of the classroom or the ward. Out of surveillance, governmentality and so on emerges the "authentic" teacher, in a rather mysterious rebirth.' Yet, for the baby room caregivers, the busy-ness of their daily lives leaves very few 'cracks' within which political dialogue and challenge can flourish. Opportunities are rare for *critically* reflecting together on the purposes and nature of their practice in both locally situated and broadly structured terms that Mac Naughton (2005, 210) suggests can 'introduce change into the larger structure of power in which our work is embedded'.

And while the spheres of influence that the caregivers cite continue to oppress, a systemic neglect to provide chances to develop critical consciousness compounds the oppression. Meanwhile, if we sit back and avoid engaging in activities that might be construed as misguided attempts to rescue caregivers 'from the iron cage', then do we also collude in their oppression?

Without significant changes to broad concepts and structures that have positioned baby room practice as 'the lowest of the low', this presents a dilemma for professional development: how to offer enriching, empowering, critically reflective and dialogic experiences while acknowledging the dangers of exposing the participants to hitherto unrecognised discourses of inadequacy or opening the doors to technicist practice and strategic compliance. Manning-Morton (2006, 48) advocates a space in which participants may:

> ... engage with the more difficult aspects of children's learning and development ... and also [to] become experts in themselves, including their own darker side. They need to be able to look at their own motivations and understand where they come from and through the knowledge they gain about themselves to better understand and adjust their responses to children. (ibid., 48)

Rather than supporting the continuation of parallel discourses, fuelled by the dislocation of practice and neglect of professional development for baby room caregivers, the provision of opportunities to develop critical consciousness concerning inherent contradictions and conflicts may help them to find their own sense of powerfulness and identity (Rockel 2009) in the broad context of sociopolitical concepts, structures and processes for early childhood education and care. But equally, and reciprocally, those of us whose gaze falls upon the baby rooms need to assess the implications of our own discourses and demands and perhaps recognise first that our expertise is 'provisional and tentative' (Brooker 2010, 195); and second that we might bring more privileged voices to the 'spheres of influence' as "people with power' and a further source of exploitation in making demands on their [baby room caregivers'] time' (Elfer 2006, 86). This raises questions for the design and conduct of both research and development activities, particularly those that may (appear to) be imposed rather than collaborative. In positioning ourselves as learners alongside participants, to what extent might we be able to engage in mutually enriching dialogic encounters so as to avoid Freire's charge that:

> The invaders penetrate the cultural context of another group, in disrespect of the latter's potentialities; they impose their own view of the world upon those they invade ... the invaders mold; those they invade are molded. (1970, 133)

The Baby Room project has tried to provide a small group of caregivers with opportunities for learning, sharing and reflection *alongside* the researchers. The findings raise a number of ethical issues. In addition to the difficulties of providing professional development opportunities that value and empower participants rather than compounding their feelings of oppressive interference, there are the ethics concerned with foregrounding babies' experiences of daycare and the employment conditions of staff. In particular, without access to professional development or dialogue, sensitive to the micro and macro politics of their working lives, the baby rooms may continue to reflect a parallel world in which caregivers' views are devalued and overridden and the 'babies best interests' are subordinated to the demands of onlookers whose voices are privileged.

Acknowledgement

The authors would like to acknowledge the generous support of the Esmée Fairbairn Foundation, which has funded the Baby Room Project since 2009.

References

Adams, M., L.A. Bell, and P. Griffin. 2007. *Teaching for diversity and social justice*. New York: Routledge.

Ailwood, J. 2008. Learning or earning in the 'smart state': changing tactics for governing early childhood. *Childhood* 15: 535–51.

Ainsworth, M.S. 1979. Infant–mother attachment. *American Psychologist*. 34, no. 10: 932–7.

Alderman, H., and E. Vegas. 2011. The convergence of equity and efficiency in ECD programs. In *No small matter: The interaction of poverty, shocks, and human capital investments in early childhood development*, ed. H. Alderman, 155–83. New York: World Bank.

Athey, C. 1990. *extending thought in young children: a parent–teacher partnership*. London: Paul Chapman.

Baldock, P., D. Fitzgerald, and J. Kay. 2009. *Understanding early years policy*. 2nd ed. London: Sage Publications.

Ball, S.J. 2003. The teacher's soul and the terrors of performativity. *Journal of Education Policy* 18, no. 2: 215–28.

Ball, S.J. 2006. *Education policy and social class: the selected works of Stephen J. Ball*. Abingdon: Routledge.

Barrett, M. 1980. *Women's oppression today: problems in Marxist feminist analysis*. London: Verso.

Belsky, J. 2009. *Effects of child care on child development: Give parents real choice*. London: Birkbeck University of London. http://www.mpsv.cz/files/clanky/6640/9_Jay_Belsky_EN.pdf (accessed May 2011).

Bowlby, J. 1988. *A secure base*. New York: Basic Books.

Brooker, L. 2010. Constructing the triangle of care: power and professionalism in practitioner/parent relationships. *British Journal of Educational Studies* 58, no. 2: 181–96.

Chanfreau, J., S. Gowland, Z. Lancaster, E. Poole, S. Tipping, and M. Toomse. 2011. *Maternity and Paternity Rights Survey and Women Returners Survey 2009/10*. London: Department for Work and Pensions.

Colley, H. 2006. Learning to labour with feeling: class, gender and emotion in childcare education and training. *Contemporary Issues in Early Childhood* 7, no. 1: 15–29.

Department for Children, Schools and Families (DCSF). 2008. *Statutory framework for the Early Years Foundation Stage*. Revised ed. Nottingham: DCSF Publications.

Department for Education (DfE). 2011. *Supporting families in the foundation years*. London: DfE Publications.

Department for Education (DfE). 2012. *Statutory framework for the Early Years Foundation Stage*. Revised version. http://www.education.gov.uk/schools/teachingandlearning/curriculum/a0068102/early-years-foundation-stage-eyfs

Durrant, J. 2010. *Evaluation of the Baby Room Project 2009–2010*. Report to the Esmée Fairbairn Foundation. Canterbury: Centre for Educational Leadership and School Improvement.

Elfer, P. 2006. Exploring children's expressions of attachment in nursery. *European Early Childhood Education Research Journal* 14, no. 2: 81–95.

Elfer, P. 2007. What are nurseries for? The concept of primary task and its application in differentiating roles and tasks in nurseries *Journal of Early Childhood Research* 5, no. 2: 169–88.

Field, J. 2008. Identity, emotions and learning in the new economy: researching call centre workers. Paper presented at the Life History Network Conference European Society for Research in the Education of Adults, Canterbury Christ Church University, March 6–9.

Figger, F., and S. Schaltegger. 2000. *What is 'stakeholder value'?* Lüneburg: University of Lüneburg in association with the United Nations Environment Programme.

Francis, B. 2001. Commonality and difference? Attempts to escape from theoretical dualisms in emancipatory research in education. *International Studies in Sociology of Education* 11, no. 2: 157–72.

Freire, P. 1970. *Pedagogy of the oppressed*, trans. Myra Bergman Ramos. London: Penguin.

Giddens, A. 1984. *The constitution of society: outline of the theory of structuration*. Cambridge: Polity Press.

Gleeson, D., and D. Knights. 2006. Challenging dualism: public professionalism in 'troubled' times. *Sociology* 40: 277–95.

Goouch, K. 2008. Understanding playful pedagogies, play narratives and play spaces. *Early Years* 28, no. 1: 93–102.

Goouch, K., and S. Powell. 2010. The baby room: looking at how we care for babies – from South East England to Shanghai. *Nursery World*, September.

Goouch, K., and S. Powell. Forthcoming, 2013. *The baby room: principles, policies and practice*. Maidenhead: Open University Press.

Hargreaves, L., and B. Hopper. 2006. Early years, low status? Early years teachers' perceptions of their occupational status. *Early Years* 26, no. 2: 171–86.

Humm, M. 1995. *The dictionary of feminist theory*. 2nd ed. London: Prentice Hall.

Kaga, Y., J. Bennett, and P. Moss. 2010. *Caring and learning together: a cross national study on the integration of early childhood care and education within education*. Paris: UNESCO.

Kröger, T. 2011. Defamilisation, dedomestication and care policy: comparing childcare service provisions of welfare states. *International Journal of Sociology and Social Policy* 31, no. 7: 424–40.

Lacey, C. 1977. *The socialization of teachers: contemporary sociology of the school*. London: Methuen.

Laevers, F. 1998. *The Leuven Involvement Scale for Young Children Manual*. Experiential Education Series Number 1. Leuven: Centre for Experiential Education.

Laevers, F. 2005. *Well-being and involvement in care settings: a process-oriented self-evaluation instrument for care settings manual*. Leuven: Research Centre for Experiential Education.

Lash, M., and M. McMullen. 2008. The child care trilemma: how moral orientations influence the field. *Contemporary Issues in Early Childhood* 9, no. 1: 36–48.

Lee, R.T., and C.M. Brotheridge. 2011. Words from the heart speak to the heart: a study of deep acting, faking, and hiding among child care workers. *Career Development International* 16, no. 4: 401–20.

Mac Naughton, G. 2005. *Doing Foucault in early childhood studies*. London: Routledge.

Manning-Morton, J. 2006. The personal is professional: professionalism and the birth to threes practitioner. *Contemporary Issues in Early Childhood* 7, no. 1: 42–52.

Moss, P. 2006. Structures, understandings and discourses: possibilities for re-envisioning the early childhood worker. *Contemporary Issues in Early Childhood* 7, no. 1: 30–41.

Moyles, J. 2001. Passion, paradox and professionalism in early years education. *Early Years: A Journal of International Research and Development* 21, no. 2: 81–95.

Nutbrown, C. 2012. *Review of early education and childcare qualifications*. Interim Report, March 2012. London: Department for Education.

Osgood, J. 2006a. Deconstructing professionalism in early childhood education: resisting the regulatory gaze. *Contemporary Issues in Early Childhood* 7, no. 1: 5–14.

Osgood, J. 2006b. Professionalism and performativity: the feminist challenge facing early years practitioners. *Early Years* 26, no. 2: 187–99.

Osgood, J. 2006c. Rethinking 'professionalism' in the early years: perspectives from the United Kingdom. *Contemporary Issues in Early Childhood* 7, no. 2: 1–4.

Osgood, J. 2010. Reconstructing professionalism in ECEC: the case for the 'critically reflective emotional professional'. *Early Years* 30, no. 2: 119–33.

Osgood, J. 2012. *Narratives from the nursery: negotiating professional identities in early childhood*. London: Routledge.

Penn, H. 2008. *Understanding early childhood: issues and controversies*. 2nd ed. Maidenhead: Open University Press.

Peters, M., and C. Lankshear. 1994. Education and hermeneutics: a Freirean interpretation. In *Politics of liberation: paths from Freire*, ed. P.L. McLaren and C. Lankshear, 173–82. London: Routledge.

Powell, S. 2010. Hide and seek: values in early childhood education and care. *British Journal of Educational Studies* 58, no. 2: 213–29.

Powell, S., and K. Goouch. 2011. Overlooked in the baby room? *Early Education*, 7–9. Spring.

Recchia, S.L., and M. Shin. 2010. 'Baby teachers': how pre-service early childhood students transform their conceptions of teaching and learning through an infant practicum. *Early Years* 30, no. 2: 135–45.

Rockel, J. 2009. A pedagogy of care: moving beyond the margins of managing work and minding babies. *Australasian Journal of Early Childhood* 34, no. 3: 1–8.

Sachs, J. 2003. *Teacher activism: mobilising the profession.* Nottingham: British Educational Research Association.

Save the Children and the Daycare Trust. 2011. *The childcare trap: making work pay.* London: Save the Children.

Schore, A.N. 2001. Effects of a secure attachment relationship on right brain development, affect regulation, and infant mental health. *Infant Mental Health Journal* 22, no. 1–2: 7–67.

Smith, R., E. Poole, J. Perry, I. Wollny, J. Reeves, C. Coshall, and J. d'Souza. 2010. *Childcare and early years survey of parents 2009.* Nottingham: DCSF Publications.

Stones, R. 2005. *Structuration theory.* Basingstoke: Palgrave Macmillan.

Stronach, I., B. Corbin, O. McNamara, S. Stark, and T. Warne. 2002. Towards an uncertain politics of professionalism: Teacher and nurse identities in flux. *Journal of Education Policy* 17, no. 1: 109–38.

Emotion in nursery work: Work Discussion as a model of critical professional reflection

Peter Elfer

Department of Education, Froebel College, University of Roehampton, London, UK

The importance of attention to children's emotions has been emphasised widely in early care and education research and policy. Enabling such attention has been seen as achieved primarily through attachment interactions with nursery staff. However, there is increasing awareness that faciltiating such interactions in a way that is optimal for children depends in part on staff's critical professional reflection about how these interactions are managed with children, with family members and between staff themselves. Such professional reflection is seen as needing to include attention to the emotional experience of staff as well as children. This paper reports on Work Discussion as a model of professional reflection that is attentive to emotional experience as it is evoked in professional work. Work Discussion and its theoretical underpinning, a psychoanalytic view of organisational ethos and interaction, is introduced and explained. The paper then reports on a Work Discussion group with nine nursery managers, the issues brought for discussion, the managers' reports of their experience of the group, and the value of Work Discussion in helping them think about and manage interactions in their nurseries.

Introduction

Attachment-based interactions in nursery

The importance for young children of their emotional experience at nursery as a central part of the goals of emotional well-being, confident playful exploration, effective thinking and learning, making friends and participating in groups is now widely accepted in early years care and education policy in England and Wales (DfES 2007; DoE 2011). These goals have largely been seen as achieved through nursery practitioners' interactions with children. Emphasis has been given in these interactions to the importance of children's opportunities to make attachments to one or two particular practitioners who can be available to the child in as sensitive, consistent and responsive a way as possible (Brooks-Gunn, Sidle-Fuligni and Berlin 2003). The importance of attachment interactions has been given progressive emphasis in the last 20 years, first as broad guidance (DoH 1991), then as specific expectation (DfES 2002), and most recently as a statutory requirement (DfES 2007; DoE 2011). The value of attachments has also been emphasised in policy frameworks or called for in many European countries (OECD 2006), in the United

States (Clarke-Stewart and Allhusen 2005), and in Australia (Ebbeck and Yim 2009).

Dual socialisation

Despite this widespread call for attachments in nursery, the approach has raised significant questions. Dahlberg, Moss and Pence (first published in 1999 [2007]) argue that the emphasis on nursery attachments is rooted in an unwarranted and unnecessary extension of attachment theory from the family to the nursery. They argue that nursery is an opportunity to facilitate children's opportunities for interactions with peers, in friendships and in groups, complementary to, but different from the emphasis on attachment interactions with adults at home. This has been referred to as the 'dual socialization' argument (Dencik 1989) referring to the value for children of participation in the two quite different social worlds of home and nursery, rather than seeking to make nursery an attachment-based extension of home. Others call for recognition that relatively short-term nursery attachments, constructed as professional interventions, cannot be simply modelled on family attachments which have lifetime trajectories and where important cultural variation exists and must be respected (Lee 2006; Degotardi and Pearson 2009; Brooker 2010).

The emotional demands of nursery interactions

However nursery attachments are conceptualised and prioritised, and whatever their emotional impact for practitioners, there is a wider discussion in the literature about the emotional demands of nursery interactions in general. One area of discussion draws on Hochschild's seminal work on 'emotional labour' (1983).

The concept is vividly illustrated by the examples of the emotional work done by debt collectors (to evoke fear in those who owe money and to suppress any feelings of sympathy they may have for the debtor's situation). For flight attendants the emotional labour lies in having to evoke positive feelings in passengers of being welcomed and valued and to suppress feelings of boredom, irritation or dislike of demanding or excessively critical passengers (Rustin 2003).

Emotional labour in nursery contexts is ubiquitous:

> Nursery staff spoke of minimising possible feelings of exclusion, guilt or envy in parents by careful control of information given to them about their child's day…. Staff were required to smile and look cheerful when parents were being shown around. There was also the labour of managing emotions evoked by parents, sometimes nursery staff being idealised as 'loving children and having endless patience' when this was far from the subjective reality. (Elfer 2008, 365)

In addition to this, it is not difficult to imagine the emotional labour of staff in seeking to suppress or evoke particular emotions with colleagues as well as parents as they are exhorted to work 'together' in an integrated and harmonious way. The early years' workforce is diverse and practitioners may experience having to work hard to submerge conflict arising from diverse cultural values and expectations regarding close relationships with children, different trainings and different conditions of service. The value of Hochschild's account is in showing that, unlike physical or mental work, emotional labour is often unacknowledged and unvalued, being understood instead as arising from the 'natural dispositions' of 'good' staff (Osgood 2004; Taggart 2011).

Alongside this literature drawing on emotional labour in relation to nursery work, there is another area of discussion from a quite different theoretical perspective concerning the work required to *contain*, rather than *evoke* emotion in nursery interactions. Historically, there has been some evidence that warm emotional engagements with children may be avoided, though not because of the emotional labour they entail to manufacture feelings of warmth where they are not felt instinctively. Rather, such engagements are seen as avoided because of anxiety that instinctive feelings of attachment to children will result in too much emotion entailing painful separations when these inevitably occur (Bain and Barnett 1986; Hopkins 1988). My own research (Elfer 2008) has proposed this as one possible explanation for the absence of individual attention even in nurseries that say they are committed to working in this way. Other recent research has also noted the absence of individual attention to children in nurseries where there was a policy commitment to it (Datler, Datler and Funder 2010; Drugli and Undheim. 2011). It is likely that other factors alongside fear of loss in close attachments may be complicit in this aspect of emotional experience at work. These have been briefly reviewed elsewhere (Elfer and Dearnley 2007) but include anxiety about the appropriateness of attachments in professional work with young children and anxiety about parents' reactions to nursery staff forming close relationships to their children.

Professional reflection taking account of emotional experience

If the emotional demands of close interactions in nursery, whether arising from close interactions with family members or practitioners or from deep feelings in relation to infants and young children, are an explicit part of professional nursery work experience, then a forum in which practitioners can talk about these feelings without fear of criticism or blame may be helpful in managing them. A case can be made that practitioners, expected and wanting to form emotionally close engagements with particular children for whom they have been allocated responsibility, should have an opportunity to talk through the emotional demands of such work. Other writers have also concluded that there is a need for forms of professional reflection in early years practice that can include critical attention to the influence of personal emotion in professional practice (Robinson 2003, 157; Manning Morton 2006).

However, there is also a case that if children are subject to an approach that seeks to encourage close emotional interaction, then from the point of view of individual children and families such interactions should be open and subject to review by the nursery collectively and in close partnership with parents. The danger of the absence of such a forum is that close relationships are implemented or avoided in ways that are considered as effectively private, because of their personal nature, and are 'off limits' to the scrutiny and accountability that is necessary in a professional context. It is difficult to see how an approach can be defended where practitioners intuitively conduct their interactions with children, or avoid interaction, influenced by patterns of interaction in their own childhoods with little systematic attention to the appropriateness of these in the context of nursery rather than family, and without any attention to the different cultural practices of different families and communities (Degotardi and Pearson 2009; Brooker 2010).

There is a second rationale for adopting emotionally attuned forms of professional reflection. The term 'Dual Socialisation' raises a number of significant questions. Its literal meaning suggests two socially polarised worlds where children experience attachment to adults in one and interactions with friends and in groups in the other, the two worlds connected by close communications between the adults who inhabit each. Yet in practice, such a polarisation is extremely unlikely in any policy context. Important questions are raised therefore about how practitioners might make emotionally sensitive and thoughtful judgements about the balance to be struck between opportunities for attachment and opportunities for peer interaction and how these two might be interactive. Further, data are needed on how this balance might be optimal for infants or toddlers compared with three- and four-year-olds and how it might vary in different nursery contexts.

Thus professional reflection might be seen as having two interrelated functions, to be *heuristic* in relation to relationship theory and practice in nursery and to be *emotionally containing* of stress and anxiety arising from emotionally close and serial engagements with young children. Further, such a forum should provide a space for the voices of nursery practitioners themselves as a key constituency in a wider democratic discussion about nursery relationship policy in particular societies and cultural contexts. The aim of this paper is therefore to propose Work Discussion as one such model of professional reflection. The paper will first briefly review the model, its theoretical underpinning and its perceived potential benefits. It will then describe the content of issues brought to the Work Discussion group by the nursery managers and their reports of their experience as they disclosed and discussed these issues with other managers. Finally, it will report on these managers' thoughts and reflections on the possible value of the WD group to enable them to think about and manage interactions within their nursery more effectively.

Work Discussion and its theoretical underpinning

This paper builds on earlier work reported in this journal (Elfer and Dearnley 2007) on the role of Work Discussion (WD) as one form of professional reflection forum. WD has a particular meaning, beyond its obvious literal sense, of a professional group process whose task is:

> ... not only of understanding what is going on, and the emotions and anxieties that are in play in a situation, but also of actively trying to help a participant observer to cope better with a situation and, through this, to enable practice to become more thoughtful. (Rustin 2008, 269)

This model of attention to work experience has been developed in a number of different disciplines and professional areas including general practitioners (Balint 1964), teachers (Jackson 2008), health workers (Hinshelwood and Skogstad 2000), and other professional workers (Rustin and Bradley 2008). The aim is to assist professionals to manage the inherent stress of their work better, and to facilitate professional reflection. Evaluations of WD in these contexts have tended to rely on self-reports of those participating concerning their perception of how helpful the groups have been in reviewing their practice. These reports, convincing in their rich accounts but limited in validity and reliability, have been positive, with reported reductions in absenteeism as a result of illness and 'above all, teachers comment on what a relief it is to discover that they are not alone in struggling with a particular difficulty...' (Jackson 2008, 79). The wider application of WD to addressing the implications for organisation design arising from the work experience of members of the organisation is at an early stage (Rustin 2008). There is a clear research agenda to develop more extensive and systematic methods of recording WD processes and outcomes (Rustin 2008, 268).

The theoretical underpinning of WD is psychoanalytic theory and the way ordinary human defences may lead professionals to avoid aspects of their work that they experience as upsetting or anxiety provoking. The aim of WD is to provide a carefully structured and facilitated forum where work experience can be sensitively thought about and practices questioned in a way that is attentive to underlying emotion and individual experience. Facilitators pay careful attention to not only what is openly said but what may appear to lie just beneath the surface of discussion.

In the earlier work reported (Elfer and Dearnley 2007), managers participated in research sessions lasting five hours each over four separate days held during one term and employing a combination of teaching and WD. In the research reported here, managers participated in two-hour discussion sessions held monthly for 10 months during one whole year. Managers took turns to present an issue and there was no teaching input. This paper reports on the issues brought for discussion and the managers' evaluations of the process.

Methodology

Twelve nursery managers in a South East England Education Authority, who had expressed interest in participating in group discussions before, were invited by the senior adviser to participate in a monthly WD with an assurance that participation was voluntary.

Following an introductory meeting in which WD was explained, these managers were given a month in which to consider whether they wished to participate. Nine agreed to do so, signing consent forms in which they agreed to keep the discussions confidential. They also agreed to keep a monthly diary of prominent events or issues in their nursery.

The WD sessions were led by two facilitators, the researcher and a second person with group relations training. Two managers presented an issue at each meeting from March to December 2010 (nine meetings in all excluding August). A written description of the issue was circulated to the group members and then read by the presenting manager. Some questions of clarification were asked by one of the facilitators. The presenter was then asked to sit listening but not contributing whilst the group discussed the issue, contributing their individual perspectives. After some 10 to 15 minutes, the presenter was invited to re-join the discussion and comment on what she had heard and her further thoughts in light of the discussion. The facilitators sensitively drew the attention of the group to possible underlying emotion in the discussion and aspects that appeared to have been avoided in discussion.

Immediately after each WD session, the facilitators and LA senior adviser, without any conferring, made notes of her or his assessment of the process and progress of the discussion. Once the WD sessions were completed in December 2010, interviews with the managers were undertaken in January/February 2011. Follow-up interviews with the senior adviser occurred in June (meeting) and July (telephone). The WD sessions were taped, fully transcribed and then coded using a grounded theory approach (Charmaz 2006) guided by four questions:

(1) What issue is being presented for discussion both in content and the form of presentation?

(2) How is the issue elucidated by the initial explorations of the group?

(3) How does the group discussion evolve, change, progress as it proceeds? What conclusions/outcomes are reached?

(4) Is there any evidence of the presenter feeling assisted in managing the issue, development of the way the presenter is thinking about the issue, or development of the way the group is thinking?

The results of this analysis were checked against the independently recorded comments of the group facilitators made immediately after each WD session. A similar approach was taken in relation to the monthly diaries maintained by the nursery managers. Here three questions were asked of the data:

(1) What are the main issues/events identified in the diary for this month?

(2) What data are there about the *way* these issues/events are presented that are indicative of management style?

(3) Are there any data that demonstrate or suggest a link between what the manager has written in the diary and what has been discussed and thought about in the WD group?

Finally, the manager interviews were also recorded and transcribed and then analysed for any comments made about the WD process and outcomes. These three sets of data were then brought together to allow themes to be discerned; five themes were identified and these are reported later in the paper.

Findings

Sixty-five monthly diaries were returned, typically two to four pages of handwritten reflections written spontaneously and with the style of a free-flowing, narrative account without too much editing. These provided rich data concerning daily life in these nurseries and an invaluable context for the issues brought for discussion.

The diaries showed how each of the nurseries operated within closely networked communities where staff often had friendship and sometimes kinship relationships with one another as well as with parents. As colleagues worked alongside each other in close proximity, personal information was exchanged easily and readily. In these close working relationships emotion appeared easily magnified. Strong camaraderie brought many benefits such as collaboration and mutual support. Staff were described as often exceptionally generous in covering another's sickness or other sudden demands on the nursery. However, in this internal community, often referred to by the managers as the 'nursery family', any tensions in staff relations also easily became magnified in their impact on nursery life.

Of the eighteen issues chosen by the managers for WD, nearly all concerned problematic or upsetting situations to do with staff rather than issues to do with children directly. The issues presented included, for example, over-dependence of staff on the guidance of managers, staff preoccupation at work with personal home issues, excessive absenteeism and breaches of procedures. The common theme, however, was suggested by the fact that managers often found themselves experiencing feelings of parental responsibility for staff.

Five themes are drawn from the analysis of the data:

(i) The collective power of a committed group of professionals to enable thinking about, rather than avoidance of, difficult emotion and its impact on professional practice

As in the diaries, the WD sessions revealed considerable levels of painful emotion impacting on work interactions. Some of this was rooted in home life but impacted at work (for example relationship breakdown, bereavement and family illness) and some had its origins in the work (for example breaches of safety or confidentiality procedures, absenteeism, over-dependence on manager guidance or subversion of manager authority). It is important not to allow the WD data to convey a picture of overwhelming unresolved conflict. The diaries showed how much emotion was mediated by managers with impressive sensitivity, firmness and personal resilience. The issues brought for WD were the ones that had proved most problematic and intractable.

For example, one manager spoke about the return of a staff member some five weeks after the suicide of this staff member's brother. The staff member did not wish to discuss this tragedy with anyone in the nursery but insisted she was 'better off' working. In presenting the issue, the manager said that the staff member's work was 'absolutely fine'. There followed a long discussion about whether someone who had experienced the suicide of a close relative could possibly be managing adequately at work. The question for the group, however, was not whether the staff member was indeed managing 'absolutely fine', which the group was not in a position to judge. Rather, the task of the group was to help the manager think about why she had brought this issue forward to begin with, if she believed that the staff member was managing 'absolutely fine'. It seemed as if the manager might actually have a doubt about this staff member's performance, which was avoided because of the sensitivity of the situation. Through the containment provided by the group, the staff member's performance at work and the difficulty of managing this problem could be thought about and possible actions considered rather than concealed as 'absolutely fine'.

(ii) The pressure to be positive for fear of a spiral of despair

The managers acknowledged a consistent pressure to keep the atmosphere cheerful both in their nurseries and in the WD:

> ... this may sound trivial, we have a whole staff mtg every 6 weeks from 6–8 p.m. but I cannot remember a time when everybody has been able to attend ... there is always person off for birthday or prior arrangement ... it IS part of their contract so why do I feel bad about discussing absences with them.... I know I am sounding bitter, however they are given at least 4w notice.... I try to start and end positively. (M9-5/2010 WD)

It often seemed as if being angry or admitting to any negative feeling could trigger a 'spiral of despair' regarding the difficulties and challenges of the work. Linked to this was a second group dynamic where managers were expected to resolve any problem or manage any situation. Managers were expected, and often expected of themselves, to be omnipotent.

As the tendency of the group to move quickly away from contentious areas of experience in the nursery and the possible value of discussing rather than avoiding these emerged, the implications of a relentlessly 'cheerful' nursery environment for children became better appreciated. Managers began to question whether they did give sufficient attention to children's negative emotion. There were examples of greater readiness to allow children to talk about or represent, in their drawings and play, experiences of loss (the loss of a friend leaving nursery, or the death of a pet) or more serious experiences to do with family relationships.

(iii) The emotional experience of being a manager: satisfaction but also guilt and loneliness

Managers said they often had to ask staff to undertake additional tasks (extra hours or shifts, or additional recording and assessment work) for very low or no pay. Conversely, sending someone home who was not fit to work may mean that person lost pay. Managers understandably felt guilty about this. Professional roles and personal relationships easily became intertwined:

> I think it's because we end up knowing so much about each other's lives sometimes whether it's because you are so close knit, as you say you build up these relationships with each other ... you are caring, you are there to support each other when things go wrong ... sometimes I just wish I didn't know as much as I did about the staff.... (M7-12/2010 WD)

The loneliness of management was also a compounding factor:

> ... when you are an employee, you try and find friends that you trust with your feelings at work ... when you are an employer, you can't really tell all your staff your personal things ... it's so difficult. (M9-3/2010 WD)

The managers spoke of needing to resist the temptation to confide in their staff about issues they felt should be kept confidential and not shared with staff, a problem identified by other organisational researchers:

> The absence of systems of managerial support can make for loneliness in the managers. The collusive hand of companionship is likely then to be doubly welcome, and managers' capacity to fulfil their containment and leadership functions are undermined. (Obholzer 1994, 209)

(iv) Conflict between the differing tasks and expectations of nursery – financial viability, nursery education, day care and family support

The primary task of a non-maintained nursery in a market system is to ensure financial viability – this is a prerequisite above all else. Fluctuations of supply and demand for places were a continual source of anxiety and stress for the managers as other settings in their proximity flourished or declined:

> A huge prospective nursery has been granted planning permission ... this 90 place setting will be on the opposite side of town so hopefully won't affect us too much though it is a big worry – our numbers have already been decimated by the opening of two children's centres this year.... (M4–5/2010 Diary)

Conflict also existed over the profit motive of nurseries as private enterprises. At one end of the spectrum, having to keep fees affordable meant that in some low-income areas it was difficult to ensure basic conditions of service including sick pay. At the other end of the spectrum, there were accusations that staff made profit for nursery owners but did not share in it. In both cases, the reality was more complex but when emotions were strained the motivations of staff, seeking sponsorship from the nursery for professional development, or of owners, seeking to ensure profitability, became easy to malign.

Managers struggled too with the increased emphasis by government on what were considered to be overly narrow educational outcomes and the relentless demands of curriculum planning. Mixed in with this was resentment about the amount of time children spent at nursery and the expectation by parents that nursery should not only cover working hours but also leisure time for parents.

Once again, the question for the WD group was not how to resolve conflicts between competing priorities, which are probably an inevitable feature of any enterprise. Rather it was whether a capacity could be learned within the group that could then be deployed in the nurseries, of how to engage in thinking about the attitudes, values and personal choices that underpin conflicts as an alternative to judgement and blame.

(v) Split communication, split thinking

As we listened to the issues presented month by month, it became clear how often two conflicting networks of communication were operating in the nurseries, one of what was said openly and formally and one that was covert (in private conversations or on social network sites). A young member of staff, who had given good service to the nursery, had become unreliable, depressed and taking regular periods of sick leave. This member of staff was denigrating the nursery on the internet and other staff were privately critical of her attitude and repeated absences but publicly sympathetic to her. Despite discussions, the staff member's behaviour and reliability did not improve. The manager proposed not to renew her temporary contract. The nursery staff, having been critical of the staff member, became critical of the manager and the firm line she was taking. The manager described feeling split, of feeling ineffective and 'soft' or of failing to understand the staff member's position, in short, of feeling either useless or ruthless.

In hearing and discussing this issue, the group appeared to extend this split to all managers:

> I'm going to say something very strange here as well – we are female as well, erm, and we have to recognize that there are hard-headed business women out there but most of us are not in that category. (M6-12/2010 WD)

The task of the facilitators was to call attention to this polarised view that one must be 'hard headed' or 'not in that category' and whether there might be another position for a nursery manager to take.

Did the managers value the WD?

Six of the nine managers were interviewed approximately one month after the sessions had concluded. Given that these interviews were conducted by one of the group facilitators, there is a question as to whether the managers would have felt able to give negative feedback. This can only be fully addressed in a larger research design. Nevertheless, manager evaluations can be treated with provisional confidence given their capacity to say quite clearly in the WD sessions when they did not think a discussion had been helpful. Second, a positive assessment of the impact of the WD on nursery culture and interactions was made by the LA adviser in follow up visits and discussions with the managers.

The managers broadly valued the time invested in the WD on three grounds:

- the reduction of competition between individual nurseries and sectors and of misconceptions concerning mutual resources and practices – the comforting reality that everyone experienced difficulties, albeit of different kinds;
- learning about group process and the value of giving time and thought to what is seen as 'negative', because it entails painful emotion, or is seen as too complex such that simple solutions are not readily available – there appeared to be a renewed capacity to tolerate discomfort and uncertainty; what seemed to be learned here was that difficult situations in nursery were not necessarily resolved by remaining 'cheerfully positive', when the difficulty could then continue to be corrosive and undermining, but that sometimes acknowledging these, even when no obvious solutions were immediately apparent, could serve to reduce their toxicity;
- a renewed determination to create time for themselves for reflection and mutual support and, possibly connected with this, to create time for children's autonomy and creativity in a culture of targets that at times could feel overbearing.

Discussion

The demands of nursery management in a market context

The data showed in forceful detail the challenges these managers faced and how much they accomplished. The anxiety entailed in the care of other people's children appeared acute. For a child to sustain even a minor injury can trigger extreme reactions from parents and for staff an investigation, feelings of blame and guilt. Managers had therefore to ensure vigilant attentive care, with staff rotas made up of complex mixes of part-time and sessional posts, and often paid at, or just above, the minimum wage. Yet this was only the minimum requirement. On top of this, they were subject to a continual flow of guidance, procedure and widening expectations, and to continual monitoring and measurement.

They did this by deploying high levels of personal commitment, often working unpaid hours, drawing on some equally committed staff but also having to manage some staff who had little training or experience or who were personally vulnerable. They were also reliant on the skills and unpaid time of their own family members to undertake gardening, decorating and maintenance work. In all of this, they valued their relationship with the LA advisory support service. Yet it was hard not to feel frustration at the costs for managers, in unpaid time and emotional investment, of maintaining the market system.

How this work relates to the existing literature on stress in education settings

The literature on stress is extensive and a full review is beyond the scope of this paper. Here, reference is made only to the increasing attention in the literature to the impact on public service professionals (for example teachers, social workers and probation officers) of working with broad social remedy expectations:

... head teachers are left shouldering concerns and anxieties on behalf of the wider community and professional network. Schools appeared to have been colonised by a whole series of functions which were previously assigned to other institutions including families. Concerns, for example, about a decline in social bondedness, raised in political discourse and in the media, appear to become rapidly designated as problems which schools are expected to solve. This apparent delegation of responsibility for broad social ills enables the wider society to feel absolved of responsibility.... (Tucker 2010, 73)

Other writers too (Osgood 2004; Page 2011; Taggart 2011) have begun to emphasise the importance of attention to how the deployment of altruism, care and indeed love in early years' contexts is to be maintained, and the personal costs for individuals. Tucker concludes:

... one of the risks is to the psychological health of the role holder, and by association the overall health of the organisation. A focus solely on technology, assessment and inspection ultimately runs the risk of ignoring the fact that human well-being is fundamental to the health of any organisation. (2010, 74)

The intrinsic demands of human service work, whether in schools or nurseries or elsewhere, combined with the increasing emphasis on unit cost, audit and competition, do seem to point to the importance of forums in early years work where practitioners can speak about the emotional impact of their work and critically reflect on their interactions with children and families. In a political and social policy climate where priority is given to measurable outcomes and immediate efficiencies achieved through sharp competition, it appears very difficult to foster collaboration or openness about difficulties faced or failures experienced. These were two of the main findings of this research in relation to nurseries but appear common in much commentary on education reform generally (see for example Rustin 2004; Tucker 2010).

Conclusion

This research raises an important question about how WD can be most effectively facilitated. Is rigorous critical reflection on interactions with children and families that is also sensitive to emotional experience as evoked at work best achieved by allowing participants to choose their own topics of discussion to present, even if these do not initially directly concern children? In the discussions reported in the paper, managers talked mainly about relationships between adults in the nursery and not directly about children. They clearly felt a strong need to talk about these relationships. Is this an important starting point? Or are the aims of WD better achieved by a more structured discussion in which the presenter is expected to focus directly on children? From a group relations perspective, where power and control in group interactions are important considerations, who is to control the agenda? Many of these managers expressed their frustration, sometimes sense of oppression, at the extent of external instruction and control. Respect for their choice of agenda therefore seemed important.

There is a related, but more subtle, group relations issue. To be of value, WD needs to lead to changes in professional practice. Yet change can be difficult and it may be tempting to find reasons why it is not possible. If the group facilitators take, or can be made to take, responsibility for the agenda, then they can also be made to take responsibility for the discussions and their outcomes. Absence of change can then be understood by the group participants as the responsibility of the group leaders rather than lying elsewhere.

Another issue is the challenge of keeping clear what it is reasonable to expect of WD. Reflective Supervision, whether in the form of WD or other forms of critical reflection on practice, cannot be a panacea for structural weaknesses. Many of the problems the managers faced had their roots in the workings of the nursery market, poor pay and conditions and inadequate training of staff. Nevertheless, this evaluation, notwithstanding its limitations, shows evidence of what WD may contribute to enabling managers to manage increasingly complex and demanding roles and the emotional components of these.

Acknowledgements

The author would like to express his appreciation to the LA in this study who commissioned the continuing professional development work, to the Froebel Research Committee for funding the evaluation, and to the managers who so willingly gave of precious time and personal experience. He would also like to express his sincere thanks to the LA senior adviser who facilitated the work and to the co-facilitator in the study who brought group relations expertise to the discussions. Finally, he would like to thank anonymous reviewers and the journal editors who gave valuable feedback on the paper.

References

Bain, A., and L. Barnett. 1986. *The design of a day care system in a nursery setting for children under five: An abridged version of a report of an action research project.* (Document No. 2T347). Institute of Human Relations for the Department of Health and Social Security (1975–1979). London: Tavistock Institute of Human Relations.

Balint, M. 1964. *The doctor, his patient and the illness.* London: Pitman Medical.

Brooks-Gunn, J., A. Sidle-Fuligni, and L.J. Berlin. eds. 2003. *Early child development in the 21st century: Profiles of current research initiatives.* New York: Teachers College Press.

Brooker, L. 2010. Constructing the triangle of care: Power and professionalism in practitioner/parent relationships. *British Journal of Educational Studies* 58, no. 2: 181–96.

Charmaz, K. 2006. *Constructing grounded theory: A practical guide through qualitative analysis.* London: Sage.

Clarke-Stewart, A.V., and Allhusen. 2005. *What we know about childcare.* Cambridge, MA: Harvard University Press.

Colley, H. 2006. Learning to labour with feeling: Class, gender and emotion in childcare education and training. *Contemporary Issues in Early Childhood* 7, no. 2: 15–29.

Dahlberg, G., P. Moss, and A. Pence. 2007. *Beyond Quality in Early Childhood Education and Care. Postmodern Perspectives.* 2nd ed. London: Falmer Press.

Datler, W., M. Datler, and A. Funder. 2010. Struggling against a feeling of becoming lost: A young boy's painful transition to day care. *International Journal of Infant Observation* 13, no. 1: 65–87.

Degotardi, S., and E. Pearson. 2009. Relationship theory in the nursery: Attachment and beyond. *Contemporary Issues in Early Childhood* 10, no. 2: 144–55.

Dencik, L. 1989. Growing up in the post-modern age: On the child's situation in the modern family in the modern welfare state. *Acta Sociologica* 32, no. 2: 155–80.

Department for Education and Skills. 2002. *Birth to three matters: A framework for supporting early years practitioners.* London: DfES SureStart Unit.

Department for Education and Skills. 2007. *The early years foundation stage.* London: DfES Publications.

Department of Education. 2011, July. *Response to the Tickell Review of the early years foundation stage.* London: DoE.

Department of Health. 1991. *The Children Act 1989 Guidance and Regulations, Vol. 2: Family support, day care and educational provision for young children*. London: HMSO.

Drugli, M.B., and A.M. Undheim. 2011. Relationships between young children in full time day care and their caregivers: A qualitative study of parental and caregiver perceptions. *Early Childhood Development and Care*. Published online, July 26.

Ebbeck, M., and H. Yim. 2009. Rethinking attachment: Fostering positive relationships between infants, toddlers and their primary caregivers. *Early Child Development and Care* 179, no. 7: 899–909.

Elfer, P. 2008. *Facilitating intimacy in the care of children under three attending full time nursery. Unpublished doctoral dissertation*. UK: University of East London.

Elfer, P., and D. Dearnley. 2007. Nurseries and emotional well being: Evaluating an emotionally containing model of professional development. *Early Years: An International Journal of Research and Development* 27, no. 3: 267–79.

Hinshelwood, R.D., and W. Skogstad, eds. 2000. *Observing organisations: Anxiety, defence and culture in health care*. Hove and New York: Brunner-Routledge.

Hochschild, A. 1983. *The managed heart: Commercialization of human feeling*. Berkeley: University of California Press.

Hopkins, J. 1988. Facilitating the development of intimacy between nurses and infants in day nurseries. *Early Child Development and Care* 33: 99–111.

Jackson, E. 2008. Work discussion groups in educational settings. *Journal of Child Psychotherapy* 34, no. 1: 62–82.

Leach, P. 2009. *Child care today: What we know and what we need to know*. Cambridge: Polity Press.

Lee, S. 2006. A journey to a close, secure and synchronous relationship: Infant–caregiver relationship development in a childcare context. *Journal of Early Childhood Research* 4, no. 2: 133–51.

Manning-Morton, J. 2006. The personal is professional: Professionalism and the birth to threes practitioner. *Contemporary Issues in Early Childhood* 7: 42–52.

Obholzer, A. 1994. Afterword. In *The Unconscious at Work: Individual and Organizational stress in the human services*, ed. A. Obholzer and V.Z. Roberts. London: Routledge.

Organisation for Economic Cooperation and Development. 2006. *Starting Strong II: Early childhood education and care*. Paris: OECD.

Osgood, J. 2004. Time to get down to business? The response of early years practitioners to entrepreneurial approaches to professionalism *Journal of Early Childhood Research* 2, no. 1: 5–24.

Page, J. 2011. Do mothers want professional carers to love their babies? *Journal of Early Childhood Research* 9: 310–23.

Piper, H., and H. Smith. 2003. 'Touch' in educational and child care settings: Dilemmas and responses. *British Educational Research Journal* 29, no. 6: 879–94.

Robinson, M. 2003. *From birth to one: The year of opportunity*. Buckingham: Open University Press.

Rustin, M. 2003. Learning about emotions: The Tavistock approach. *European Journal of Psychotherapy, Counselling and Health* 6, no. 3: 187–208.

Rustin, M. 2004. Rethinking audit and inspection. *Soundings* 26: 86–107.

Rustin, M. 2008. Work discussion: Implications for research and policy. In *Work discussion: Learning from reflective practice in work with children and families*, ed. M.E. Rustin and J. Bradley, 267–84. London: Karnac.

Rustin, M.E., and J. Bradley, eds. 2008. *Work discussion: Learning from reflective practice in work with children and families*. London: Karnac.

Taggart, G. 2011. Don't we care?: The ethics and emotional labour of early years professionalism. *Early Years: An International Journal of Research and Development* 31, no. 1: 85–95.

Tucker, S. 2010. An investigation of the stresses, pressures and challenges faced by primary school head teachers in a context of organisational change in schools: Stresses and challenges faced by head teachers. *Journal of Social Work Practice* 24, no. 1: 63–74.

Caregiver–child relationships as a context for continuity in child care

Susan L. Recchia

Curriculum and Teaching, Teachers College, Columbia University, New York, USA

This paper focuses on one aspect of continuity – the caregiver–child relationship – within a larger global study of continuity in child care based at a university-affiliated child care center. Case studies are presented of two toddler boys, followed as they transitioned from their infant classroom to the preschool classroom at the age of approximately 2½ years. Data from caregiver notes, developmental progress reports, coded teacher interviews, Attachment Q-Sets, and the Pianta Student–Teacher Relationship Scale (STRS) were analyzed and integrated to form case profiles to reflect the children's relationship experiences across the transition. Results are discussed in terms of individual differences in child behavior and caregiver perceptions, continuity and discontinuity factors in the transition experience, and implications for policy and practice.

Sensitive and responsive maternal care giving has long been associated with secure emotional attachments and social competence in infants and young children, with implications for positive social development throughout the lifespan (Ainsworth et al. 1978; Sroufe 1983; Erickson, Sroufe, and Egeland 1985; Berlin and Cassidy 1999). Although most of the previous theory and research has focused primarily on the mother–infant attachment relationship, more recent findings from early childhood studies support the application of attachment concepts to relationships beyond the family (Howes and Hamilton 1992; Raikes 1993; Elicker and Fortner-Wood 1995; Howes 1997, 1999; Pianta 1997; Howes, Hamilton, and Philipsen 1998). Child development experts agree that best practice in infant and toddler care-giving requires a strong focus on building positive and trusting relationships, and that this relationship-focused care-giving should have as its goal the development of secure attachments between children and their caregivers (Raikes 1996; Howes and Ritchie 2002).

Pianta and his colleagues (Pianta and Steinberg 1992; Pianta 1997) have found associations between early teacher–child relationships and children's later school experiences. Additional findings from child care studies indicate that young children's early relationships with their child care teachers may be a stronger predictor of later peer relationships than are early mother–child relationships (Howes, Matheson, and Hamilton 1997; Howes 1999). Although the types of relationships that young children form with their teachers tend to remain stable across the early years of schooling (Pianta and Steinberg 1992; Howes and Ritchie 2002), there is some evidence which suggests that toddlers, as opposed to older children, have not yet generalized their representations of teacher–child relationships, and will construct 'a new representation for each new teacher' (Howes et al. 1998, 418).

Researchers have noted similarities between the characteristics of sensitive caregiving in parents and other caregivers, and the functions which secure relationships serve both at home and in child care (Raikes 1996; Kontos and Wilcox-Herzog 1997; Howes and Ritchie 2002). Few studies, however, have focused on attachment relationships in nonlinear ways (Sander 2000), or attended to individual differences in attachment relationships over time and across contexts, particularly as they relate to continuity and change (Elicker and Fortner-Wood 1995; Seifer and Schiller 1995; Thompson 2000). Information on the relationship-building process in child care, as experienced by individual children and their caregivers, could provide useful guidelines for preparing and supporting caregivers as they enter the field (Elicker 1997). It could also have important policy implications regarding such issues as staffing, group size, and curriculum choices in child care programs (Lally 1995).

Clearly mothers and others come to the process of building relationships with infants and toddlers from somewhat different vantage points, and within very different emotional contexts. Little information is available to guide our understanding of how this process proceeds for children and out-of-home caregivers, and particularly how it might change over time. Although many infant centers promote the development of attachments between infants and caregivers by assigning primary caregivers for each child, it is not always possible to look at the 'goodness-of-fit' between the individual infant's needs and the caregivers' strengths or skills before these assignments are made (Daniel and Shapiro 1996). Furthermore, as children get older, they traditionally transition to larger groups within child care settings, with higher child to staff ratios. Primary caregiver models may be less feasible or less appropriate to implement within these groups, as children's needs and developmental competences change (Nelson and Garduque 1991; Howes 1999; Thompson 2000).

According to Elicker and Fortner-Wood (1995), variations in the nature and quality of interactions between infants and their caregivers should be expected, even in those settings in which the majority of caregivers form secure relationships with nearly all of the children. Some children may form secure attachments to their caregivers quickly and easily, while others will need more time and focus before they are able to do so (Raikes 1996). Individual differences in developmental patterns in child–caregiver relationships may also contribute to differential degrees of caregivers' felt closeness and children's secure-base behavior (Recchia et al. 2000).

The current study was designed as a preliminary exploration of aspects of continuity and discontinuity in young children's relationships with their caregivers across the transition from an infant to a preschool child care environment. Although many studies, in the US as well as internationally, have documented transition experiences for children entering child care or moving from child care into kindergarten, (Pianta, Cox, Taylor, and Early 1999; Kraft-Sayre and Pianta 2000; Dockett and Perry 2001; Margetts 2002; Ahnert et al. 2004; Fabian and Dunlap 2007; Peters 2010; Einarsdottir 2011), few have explored transitions from one room to another within a childcare setting (Recchia and Dvorakova 2012). Infants who start their center child care experience in an infant room and later move to a toddler room are a particularly interesting group to study given the significance of attachment relationships during the first 3 years of life, and the relationship-based nature of infant and toddler care (Elicker and Fortner-Wood 1995; Raikes 1996). The process of change from one room to another may present particular challenges to this age group as they face the task of developing new relationships with caregivers and peers, and adapting to new expectations in the preschool curriculum (Recchia and Dvorakova 2012).

This work is a subset of a larger, more global study which explored multiple aspects of continuity within one child care environment. The two toddler boys profiled here presented distinctive differences in their relationships with caregivers across the two settings, calling particular attention to the potential complexities of young children's and teachers' experiences building relationships in childcare. Looking qualitatively at the data sources for these participants provided an opportunity to ask deeper questions of the data. By examining the children's behavior toward their caregivers and caregivers' perceptions of their relationships with the children, we hoped to gain insight into the ways in which child–caregiver relationships may change over time and across early childhood classrooms, and how they might contribute to children's experiences of continuity in child care.

The following research questions were explored in this study: (1) How do two toddler boys respond to their new caregivers as they transition to a new classroom in child care? (2) How do the caregivers in each classroom describe their relationships with the children before, during, and after the transition process? and (3) What can we learn from children and caregivers about practices that support positive relationships across transitions in child care?

Method

Setting

This study was conducted at a university-affiliated child care program, which also serves as a training site for graduate students who are studying early childhood development and practice. Ongoing research is integrated in the work of the center, and parent permission is secured for all studies. Care was provided within inter-age classroom groupings for children aged 6 weeks to 5 years. The infant room housed children from as young as 6 weeks until they were about 2½, at which time they usually transitioned to the preschool classroom. In the infant room, group size was no larger than eight infant-toddlers at one time, with at least three adult caregivers. One head infant teacher was always present, assisted by part-time caregivers and/or student caregivers. Staffing patterns and staff–child ratios varied between the classrooms, with larger group size and higher child-to-staff ratios in the older classroom. In the preschool room, the group size could be as large as 12, with a similar number and configuration of adult staff. Preschool children ranged in age between 2½ and 5 years. Curricular variations between classrooms reflected appropriately increasing structure and social responsibilities for older children.

Participants

Two toddler boys and their caregivers within two classrooms were the primary focus for this study. Scott, a European-American boy, started in the infant room at two months, and Charles, an African-American boy, entered the infant room at 18 months. Both boys were enrolled in childcare on a part-time basis at first, increasing their hours over time. When Scott was 29 months and Charles was 28 months, they transitioned together to the preschool classroom. Although their infant teachers participated in classroom visits with the children prior to the official transition, once the transition became official the children were cared for by their new teachers. While in the infant room, the children were assigned 'key caregivers' (female graduate students working as training fellows at the center), who cared for them alongside the regular classroom staff. In the preschool classroom, students worked with the staff but children were not assigned key caregivers. The data generated for analyses came from student and staff caregivers associated with the children in each classroom. Two full-time female staff members participated in the caregiver interviews, one from each classroom.

Procedures

Attachment Q-Sort. While in the infant room, children and their key caregivers were participants in a larger study of the development of caregiver–child relationships in childcare. As a part of this study, key caregivers were observed with their key children at several time points throughout their first semester at the center. Children's attachment behavior in relation to their key caregivers was assessed using the Attachment Q-Set (AQS) (Waters 1987). The Q-sorting task was conducted by trained observers (the researcher and research assistants) after careful observation of the child–key caregiver dyad. The observer sorted 90 cards containing brief descriptions of children's behavioral responses to their caregivers into nine piles of 10 cards each, ranging from most like to most unlike the child's responses. The Q-Set was sorted for each child at two time points, once during the initial stage of care giving (week 3) and a second time near the end of the 15-week period (week 13). (For further information on Q-sort procedure and reliability, see Recchia et al. 2000.) The second set (Time 2) of Q-sort security scores for Scott and Charles were examined for this study. AQS scores were computed using a statistical program specifically for this purpose (Waters 1987). The security score is based on the correlation between the child's actual sort and an 'optimal' criterion sort. Scores can range from –1.00 to +1.00, with higher scores denoting greater security.

Student–Teacher Relationships Scale. Also as a part of the larger study, infant room student caregivers were asked to rate their key children at the second time point (week 13), using the Student–Teacher Relationship Scale (STRS) (Pianta 1996). A five-point 28-item Likert-type rating scale, the STRS yields a total positive relationship score based on teachers' perceptions of their relationships with each child scored. Two of the factor-based sub-scales on this measure were examined, Conflict (the extent to which the teacher is 'at odds' with the child), and Closeness (the degree of positive affect in the relationship). These factors are derived out of attachment theory and its behavioral correlates (Ainsworth et al. 1978).

Scores on the STRS were used to assess key caregivers' perceptions of their relationships with their key children. At the end of the semester following each child's transition into the next classroom, preschool teachers were also asked to rate the children using the STRS. The STRS sub-scales of 'Closeness' and 'Conflict' were examined for Scott and Charles in the present study. STRS scores used for this analysis were generated by the children's key caregivers in the infant room, and by the teacher who spent the most time with them in the preschool room. Both the key caregivers and the teachers completed the STRS after one semester of working with the children.

Developmental reports. In line with general procedures at the center, children's progress is described in annual developmental reports written by a student fellow or a staff member. Reports from the classrooms were reviewed for both children, highlighting information on the child–caregiver relationship. Relevant anecdotes were later integrated and triangulated with other data sources.

Student caregiver journals. Throughout their semester as key caregivers, students responded to weekly journal questions regarding the course of their relationships with their key children. These journals were reviewed for insight on the relationship-building process. Relevant anecdotes were selected for use in each case synthesis.

Caregiver interviews. Approximately 4–6 weeks after the children transitioned into the preschool classroom, a caregiver from each classroom who knew the children well was interviewed by a research fellow. Interviews lasted from 45 minutes to an hour. Caregivers were asked a few open-ended questions encouraging them to speak freely about the children's response to the transition from their points of view. Specific topics included the ways in which the infant and preschool caregivers had tried to work with the children, pre- and post-transition, respectively, and the ways in which the caregivers saw the two classrooms as the same or different. Interviews were tape recorded and transcribed and later coded for emerging themes.

Data analysis

Given the goals of this exploratory study, to look more deeply at those aspects that might contribute to potentially complex changes in relationships over time, qualitative case studies were selected as the most appropriate methodology (Denzin and Lincoln 2005). All data were integrated to contribute to the development of a 'relationship case profile' for each child (Stake 2005). Each case profile was constructed through a synthesis of information from the measures used, the children's developmental reports, and the caregiver journals and interviews (Wolcott 1994). Scores on the quantitative measures (the Q-Set and the STRS) were referenced here solely for the purpose of triangulation. Descriptive anecdotes from the developmental reports as well as quotes from the teacher interviews were selected as exemplars of the themes which emerged within each child's profile.

Results

How do the children respond to their caregivers?

Infant room behavior. While in the infant room, both Scott and Charles were observed with their key caregivers as participants in an ongoing study. Attachment Q-set scores reflecting these interactions gave insight into the degree to which the children demonstrated secure base behavior in their responses. Both boys demonstrated secure attachment behavior toward their key caregivers by the end of one semester in their care, with Scott's score of 0.65 a bit higher than Charles' score of 0.50.

Additional insights from caregiver interviews and child progress reports revealed that both boys developed positive relationships with peers and adults while in the infant room. Scott was described as 'a very social child ... [who] loves to be with other children and makes friends with them.' His report presented many examples of his initiations of play with peers. He was also seen to relate well to adults, as described by his key caregiver, who stated: 'Scott ... is also very friendly and tries to be close to caregivers.'

Charles's key caregiver described the process she went through as she got to know him in the infant room. At first she felt distant from him, expressing her frustration during the first half of the semester in the following ways: 'I feel distant from Charles because he ignores me when he's resisting doing something.... I don't know how to relate to him... [I'm] getting very frustrated with Charles, experiencing him as extremely avoidant.' Over time, however, they grew closer, and his caregiver expressed this emotional change in the following ways: 'Charles is more related which makes being with him much more enjoyable.... [He is] more affectionate and sustains interactions.... Charles continues to be more responsive and seeks me out to join him in activities.'

Preschool room behavior. Developmental reports from the preschool room describe Charles as having made an easy transition and relating well to teachers and peers. His teachers described his behavior in the following ways: 'because of C's strong social skills ... and his ability to "psych out" a setting, he was able to adapt to the new setting easily and with little apparent stress' (this despite being one of the youngest children in the room).... [He] follows most adult prompts and shows trust for both peers and caregivers.... With the smallest prompt, caregivers generally receive C's cooperation.'

For Scott, on the other hand, the transition was challenging. According to his report, 'his overall response to the change was one of stress.' Both his parents and his caregivers noted changes in his behavior. His teachers described his behavior in the following way:

> ... Scott often displayed distress when the parent who brought him to the Center tried to leave.... It frequently took up to 45 minutes to separate from his parent each day, and he would be sad, if not crying for a few minutes after that.

Scott eventually allowed a teacher to comfort him, but his relationships were strained. The following anecdotes support these findings:

> He did allow one of the teachers ... to comfort him, and introduce him to a number of the centers and materials in the room... He had an issue regarding keeping his shoes on.... After realizing the importance of this practice (it was a routine from the infant room) ... the staff began to work with him on taking the shoes off when he wished.... Scott's physical activity became more unceasing on some days ... while on other days he would be relatively inactive, more frequently seeking the comfort of an adult lap.... He did not continue to try to create relationships with other children or adults.

How do caregivers perceive their relationships with the children?

The Student Teacher Relationship Scale, like other measures of adult perceptions, assesses the teacher's emotional involvement with the child (Howes 1999). For the purpose of this paper, the Closeness and Conflict subscales of the STRS were highlighted. A comparison of overall mean scores from the larger study showed no significant differences between the infant and preschool room caregivers' ratings for the children.

An examination of the scores for Scott and Charles, however, showed an interesting change pre- and post-transition. While teacher perceptions for Scott showed increasing Conflict (from 1.9 to 2.5 on a five-point scale) and decreasing Closeness (from 3.9 to 2.7), those for Charles showed an increase in perceptions of Closeness (from 3.8 to 4.2) and a decrease in Conflict (from 2.7 to 2.0). Although these scores should be interpreted carefully as they represent only two ratings taken at specific points in time, they add trustworthiness to our qualitative findings, which reflect a corresponding directional change in the nature of the teacher–child relationships during the transition process.

What do caregivers tell us about the transition?

Transcriptions of caregivers' post-transition interviews were reviewed for emerging themes around caregiver–child relationships within the contexts of the different classroom environments. Two broad themes seemed to run through each interview: (1) expectations for child behavior as a framework for relationships within the classroom; and (2) the caregiver's role as a respondent to the child within the environment.

Expectations for child behavior. Interview comments from each caregiver referred both directly and indirectly to the idea that there was a framework within which children's behavior was interpreted in each of their classrooms. The infant room caregiver referred several times to the notion of structure, and the ways in which it was different between the two environments. She stated:

> At the [infant room] our schedule is pretty fluid. We have some structure, but the day is really very child-directed … we don't have specific times we're doing things…. If a child is on the climber and it takes him 20 minutes to try to figure out how to shift his weight from one foot to the other, I don't want anybody to bother me … because I'm watching that child. And I want that child to have all the time he needs….

The preschool room teacher also talked about differences in the structure of the environments, stating 'The rooms are so very different that it's almost a culture shock for these children coming from one room to the other….' She further elaborated on the ways in which these changes affected the two boys' experiences.

> … it became obvious very quickly that the two rooms were very different, that they were used to a very different schedule during the day. They were used to a very different routine … a different … teacher–child relationship and ratio in the classroom…. There are some things that we … because we have such a large group … can't make accommodations for. [Scott] does not like chaotic … transitions from snack to going outside and he resists and resists and resists but that's really not a choice when the children are going outside, he needs to go outside…. For naptime because all of the other children are sleeping [Scott] needs to at least attempt to stay on his mat…. We don't let him sit there for 2 hours with nothing to do, but usually about 40 minutes into it, when it becomes obvious that he's not falling asleep, we give him toys and books…. Usually we try to hold off … especially with somebody who is as young as he is, thinking that he needs his sleep and I think that he does….

The parameters of what was desirable and what could be acceptable within each classroom may have influenced both children's ways of relating to the caregivers and caregivers' perceptions of their relationships with the children. Both caregivers used terms to describe the children's behavior as 'normal or typical for their age,' as evidenced in their selected comments below. The infant room teacher had this to say:

> Every time [Scott] does something I say, well he's a two-year old. He empties. He dumps. He moves all of the time.... But Charles listens to exterior control ... you can do that verbally with Charles. But with Scott you have to do that very physically.... Charles is a little more reserved in some of the things he does ... a little bit more cautious – both physically and in his interactions with people. And in the way he will not listen to adults. He is very careful in what he chooses not to listen to; whereas Scott just doesn't listen. [laughs] – He's two!

In her descriptions of the children's behaviors shortly after the transition, the preschool room teacher expressed a sense of frustration with what she saw as Scott's difficult behaviors. It was clear from her comments that he did not easily adapt to the new classroom routines and expectations. She provided the following description of his behavior:

> [He was] kicking [and] screaming during our transition times, getting into the cart when he had to put his coat on, keeping his shoes off, keeping his socks off (which is a practice in the other classroom), trying to rile Charles up and then having that dejected stance when Charles wasn't following along with him, not eating, and not sleeping.... When he is anxious ... he gets wound up in a way that's not typical of a child, even a child who has a lot of energy.

Charles, on the other hand, more easily conformed to the new classroom routines, and his transition seemed to be viewed as a very positive experience. According to his teacher, 'Charles' transition seemed to be very smooth. He was fine separating from his parents in the morning, was ... making nice connections with the children, although he was somewhat on the periphery,' which she further described as 'normal for his age.'

Although the two boys continued to demonstrate behavioral differences as they had in the infant room, within the preschool classroom context, Scott's developmental differences seemed to be perceived as more disruptive to the daily schedule and more out of synch with the teachers' expectations. In comparing Scott with Charles, the preschool teacher shared the following observations:

> Instead of resisting the way Scott was, [Charles] was just trying to follow along.... [Scott]'s not at an age or developmental stage where he is very willing to participate in group activities. Again, totally normal, although Charles was going along with it.... [Charles is] happy to come into the room. He eats, he sleeps, he does everything nicely.... Charles has a higher, a better ability than Scott at this point to check out the social scene.

Caregiver's role as respondent to the child. The second relationship theme that emerged from the teachers' interviews was reflected in their statements regarding the ways they responded to the children within their classrooms, particularly to Scott and Charles. In the infant room, the caregiver emphasized the level of physical responding to the children in the following way:

We make a real effort to tap into the kid. And figure out what the parent wants for the kid and to mesh that … to be genuine with the children. And there's a lot of love, a lot of physical contact in the [infant room] between the child and the teacher. Children can sit on my lap. Children can lie on my back.... So there's a bond that forms because we're so intimate with each other.

She also spoke of the way in which she would play with Scott and Charles, both of whom were expecting baby siblings later in the year, before their transition into the preschool room:

I would be holding Larry (a young infant) … and Scott more than Charles … would … look at me. And I would say to them, 'Are you thinking that maybe you would like to be held by me like Larry, like a baby?' … Scott would come up behind … and not even look at you. And then I would go to hold him, he would squiggle away and I would tickle him....

During pre-transition visits with the children to the preschool room, the infant room caregiver tried to slowly introduce the boys to the routines at their own pace. She began by having them participate in circle time, an activity that was not a part of their infant classroom repertoire. She described this experience in the following way:

We would try to take part in their circle time. And then just to play. And we would let the children go there and stay as long as they could bear it. When Scott would say to me 'home'… and Charles would walk out the door, those were the signs that I knew they were ready to go back. Charles would just go! And Scott would say 'home'.

Both of the classroom caregivers spoke of changes in their relationships, particularly with Scott, after the transition. For the infant caregiver, there seemed to be a sense of loss. She described Scott's behavior as follows:

One day as I walked up the hall … he walked to the door and … he said 'goodbye Gail'. And I was like, you just want to cry you know? … He would look at me and he wouldn't come to me....

According to the preschool teacher, it took a while for Scott to accept her. 'Scott showed his stress by … crying or running away from the room, having a hard time separating from his parents in the morning, and having a hard time making attachments with the caregivers.' However, over time, her ability to reflect on her own behavior and her increased willingness to adapt her responses to him demonstrated her capacity for building a relationship with Scott:

At first we were trying to herd [Scott] into the group … then we allowed him to just play in the classroom and we have finally developed a system.... Lunch and snack times we've made optional pretty much. At lunchtime he has to sit with his friends … just so he starts getting used to the routine.... We need to make accommodations for him. I think that's it.... I've become a lot more affectionate with [Scott], which is really something he seems to enjoy and he becomes giggly and happy. He feels loved which is good, but it takes time to get to know the children.

For Charles, who easily responded to the routines and social expectations of the room, the preschool teacher reacted positively when he began to feel comfortable enough to be less compliant, further illustrating her flexibility in responding to the boys over time:

> [Charles] was following along very cautiously just trying to get a handle on things and now that he's been there a little while he's starting to resist some things, which is good. It shows that he's starting to feel more secure and developing a will and feels comfortable expressing that will in our classroom....

Discussion

Children's transition experiences have been described in the literature as a complex process (Dockett and Perry 2001) which individual children must navigate at their own pace (Recchia and Dvorakova 2012). Maintaining positive relationships with adults through the transition process is considered a central component to success (Peters 2010). Although the majority of studies have focused primarily on the transition from child care to kindergarten, where changes in the nature of the classroom structure and teacher expectations for behavior may be more striking, components regarding the importance of positive teacher–child relationships across settings might also apply to earlier transitions (Howes and Ritchie 2002). When children are less ready to make the transition into a new classroom, the transition experience can have a negative impact on their learning and self-esteem (Fabian and Dunlop 2007). Before children can reach their previous level of comfort within a new classroom, they must adapt to the physical and social features of the unfamiliar environment (Cryer et al. 2005).

For very young children like those in the current study, the role of the teacher as a source of support and comfort through the transition process may be even more significant than for older children. For many toddlers, establishing a secure relationship with at least one teacher may be a necessary component to fully realizing relationships with peers (Howes and Hamilton 1992; Recchia and Dvorakova 2012), a primary goal of preschool education. In the case of the two toddler boys profiled here, Scott had spent over 2 years in the infant classroom prior to the transition, where he had made strong connections with his caregivers, who had also shared in many phases of his physical, social, and emotional development. Charles began in the infant room at 18 months, having already achieved many developmental milestones outside of this classroom context. The degree to which Scott had formed deep relationships with his infant room caregivers may have contributed to his more difficult transition to a new classroom environment. It is also possible that the infant caregivers felt a greater sense of loss in Scott's transition, which may have inadvertently contributed to his reluctance to move on.

Two very different relationship profiles emerged for these toddler boys as they transitioned from the infant to the preschool classroom. Scott, who had spent most of his young life as a member of the infant room, referring to it as 'home,' seemed to change during the transition period. He went from a socially outgoing child who felt free and comfortable within the structure of his infant classroom to a child who appeared anxious, socially unresponsive, and unhappy with the expectations of his new caregivers and the structure of his new environment. Scott's distress in dealing with the change in turn seemed to affect his caregivers' ability to support his transition. His infant caregivers' descriptions and perceptions of their relationships with him reflected high levels of closeness and low conflict. Preschool room caregivers' descriptions and perceptions of their relationships with Scott seemed to reflect their sense of conflict in their interactions with him as well as their difficulty in establishing a close relationship with him. The free-flowing atmosphere of the infant room seemed to suit Scott's personal style of exploring his environment and relating to his teachers; however, his comfort there may have also contributed to his resistance toward the more scheduled and structured atmosphere in the preschool room.

For Charles, on the other hand, who had spent much less time in the infant room, and appeared less socially connected to his caregivers, the transition to the preschool went much more smoothly. Charles readily complied with the new teacher expectations for behavior, and appeared to assimilate into the new classroom environment quickly. The ease with which he made the transition seemed to support his new caregivers' positive descriptions and perceptions of their relationships with him.

Although both boys demonstrated secure base behaviors in the infant room in relation to their key caregivers, the transition to the preschool classroom appeared to create different levels of discontinuity for them. Charles, who was more able to assess and respond to the change in social expectations, appeared to the preschool teachers as more 'ready' for their classroom. Although he still required some period for adjusting to the changes in environment, Charles seemed able to get on board with the new expectations quite quickly. Scott, who found the discontinuities between the two environments more challenging, was less able to assimilate. His inability to adapt easily, in turn, created challenges for the caregivers, which required them to rethink their expectations for him. Although the preschool caregivers were able to work toward better accommodating Scott's needs, and to begin to slowly build a positive relationship with him, this process took time and effort. It also required the preschool teachers to make changes in their expectations for his behavior, and in their ways of responding to him. In order to help him make the adjustment to the new classroom, they needed to allow him to engage in some of the comfortable behaviors he was accustomed to in the infant room until he was more at ease in the new setting.

Thompson (2000), in discussing the role of continuity and change in parent–child attachment relationships, points out the importance of examining contextual changes in family systems, such as the birth of a new child or a parental separation, as a potential explanation for changes in the continuity of children's behavioral responses. In a sense, a child's transition from one classroom to another represents a similar kind of contextual change. Changes in familiar patterns of interaction impose a need to renegotiate relationships, potentially challenging children's emotion regulation and adaptive coping abilities. Adult reactions to these transitions also play a role in fostering continuity or discontinuity in children's relationship experiences (Cryer et al. 2005).

The final phase of Bowlby's (1969/1982) theory describes the ways in which preschool children maintain a goal-corrected partnership with their attachment figures. Maintenance of this partnership involves negotiation with caregivers in the context of conflict over sometimes opposing goals and intentions (Thompson 2000). At this stage of development, both children's needs and caregivers' expectations for behavior are changing significantly from what they were during infancy. These changes, although they may be appropriately reflected in the differences between infant and preschool childcare environments, may contribute to a greater sense of discontinuity for some transitioning children. The findings presented here corroborate those of Recchia and Dvorakova (2012), who suggest that different children need different things from their teachers to support their transitions to a new classroom. Childcare teachers who are able to take an individualized, child-centered approach, and follow the children's lead (Recchia and Loizou 2002; Recchia and Shin 2010) as they form relationships with them in the transition process, may be better able to accommodate the diverse ways that children experience and cope with challenging changes in their classroom environments.

Scott and Charles represent two very different constellations of relationship change during the transition from infancy to preschool. Although both boys were able eventually to form positive relationships with their new caregivers, the relationship process took its own form in each case. Transition has the potential to create discontinuity, but as this study showed, adaptable and sensitive care-giving can ameliorate challenges to the transition process. Findings from the multiple sources of data used to create the relationship profiles presented here provide insight into the strengths and needs of the children, as well as the challenges for caregivers in supporting the development of positive relationships in child care. These findings also demonstrate the ways that children both contribute to the transition process and teach us about it (Dockett and Perry 2001).

Implications for caregiver training and program policy

Children and their caregivers each bring their own strengths and expectations to the process of building relationships. As classroom contexts change, interactive styles, which foster secure relationships, may change as well. Assigning key caregivers in an infant classroom, where the focus falls more naturally toward the individual, seems to foster the growth of positive relationships. However, this system does not always work smoothly, as child–caregiver dyads are not all easy matches (Recchia and Shin 2010). Some caregivers perceive greater closeness in their relationships with non-key children, and some children are more difficult to get close to than others (Recchia et al. 2000). Relationship building is a dynamic process, which requires time, patience, flexibility, and commitment. As children move into preschool classrooms, their developing social competences and skills may require different kinds of support from teachers (Howes 1999; Recchia and Dvorakova 2012). Teachers' expectations and classroom structures may also preclude an individual focus on children. However, as evidenced in Scott's profile, sometimes children's needs require adaptations to the classroom structure during the transition period to promote the relationship-building process.

Promoting positive caregiver–child relationships in early educational environments requires attention to many aspects of the care-giving context. Group size, caregiver–child ratios, caregiver expectations and responsibilities, caregiver flexibility, and the nature of classroom activities may each have a powerful impact on the relationship experiences of children and their caregivers (Cryer et al. 2005). If building positive relationships with children in childcare is to be a priority, adjustments within each of these areas may need to be made, especially as children make transitions from one classroom to another. It seems particularly important for caregivers to act as a bridge for children who are newly entering their classrooms, building on children's previous experiences to the extent possible, and allowing them to ease in to the new environment. However, the transition can also be supported in particular ways by the sending caregivers, who can work within their firmly established relationships with the children to help them anticipate the changes in the new classroom. Most children are able to adjust to change over time, and the challenges brought by the discontinuities of transition can ultimately encourage children's positive growth and development (Recchia and Dvorakova 2012). However, having support from their sending caregivers who already know them well, and their new caregivers who are able to invest in getting to know and form individual relationships with them as they enter their new classrooms, can have an impact on children's immediate social and emotional experiences, as well as their future experiences in school (Howes and Ritchie 2002).

This study used multiple measures in an attempt to explore a dynamic and complex issue, continuity in teacher–child relationships across classroom transitions, in a comprehensive and integrated way. In order to promote relationship continuity, teachers need administrative support as they struggle with personally challenging relationships in childcare during periods of possible discontinuity. Children need time and space to move through the transition process encouraged by caring adults. Although this study explored the experiences of only two children, the findings raise interesting questions for future research regarding the contributions of child behavior, caregiver perceptions and responses, and classroom structures to a fuller understanding of the dynamics of caregiver–child relationships in child care (Recchia and Shin 2010). These findings can inform child care policy and professional practice for both caregivers and their supervisors.

References

Ahnert, L., M.R. Gunnar, M.E. Lamb, and M. Barthel. 2004. Transition to child care: Associations with infant–mother attachment, infant negative emotion, and cortisol elevations. *Child Development* 75: 639–50.

Ainsworth, M.D.S., M. Blehar, E. Waters, and S. Wall. 1978. *Patterns of attachment.* Hillsdale, NJ: Erlbaum.

Berlin, L.J., and J. Cassidy. 1999. Relations among relationships: Contributions from attachment theory and research. In *Handbook of attachment*, ed. J. Cassidy and P. Shaver, 688–712. New York: Guilford Press.

Bowlby, J. 1969/1982. *Attachment and loss* (Vol. 1). 2nd ed. New York: Basic Books.

Cryer, D., L. Wagner-Moore, M. Burchinala, N. Yazejiana, S. Hurwitza, and M. Woleryb. 2005. Effects of transitions to new child care classes on infant/toddler distress and behavior. *Early Childhood Research Quarterly* 20: 37–56.

Daniel, J., and J. Shapiro. 1996. Infant transitions: Home to center-based childcare. *Child and Youth Care Forum* 25, no. 2: 111–23.

Denzin, N.K., and Y.S. Lincoln. 2005. *The Sage handbook of qualitative research.* Thousand Oaks, CA: Sage Publications.

Dockett, S., and B. Perry. 2001. Starting school: Effective transitions. *Early Childhood Research and Practice* 3, no. 32. http://ecrp.uiuc.edu/v3n2/dockett.html.

Einarsdottir, J. 2011. Icelandic children's early education transition experiences. *Early Education and Development* 22, no. 5: 737–56.

Elicker, J. 1997. Introduction to the special issue: Developing a relationship perspective in early childhood research. *Early Education and Development* 8, no. 1: 5–10.

Elicker, J., and C. Fortner-Wood. 1995. Adult–child relationships in early childhood programs. *Young Children* 51, no. 1: 69–78.

Erickson, M.F., L.A. Sroufe, and B. Egeland. 1985. The relationship between quality of attachment and behavior problems in preschool in a high-risk sample. In *Growing points in attachment theory and research*, ed. I. Bretherton and E. Waters. Monographs of the Society for Research in Child Development, 50, no. 1–2: Series No. 209.

Fabian, H., and A. Dunlop. 2007. Outcome of good practices in transition processes for children entering primary school. *Paper commissioned for the EFA Global Monitoring Report 2007, Strong foundations: Early childhood care and education.* Paris: UNESCO.

Howes, C. 1997. Teacher sensitivity, children's attachment and play with peers. *Early Education and Development* 8, no. 1: 41–9.

Howes, C. 1999. Attachment relationships in the context of multiple caregivers. In *Handbook of attachment*, ed. J. Cassidy and P. Shaver, 671–87. New York: Guilford Press.

Howes, C., and C.E. Hamilton. 1992. Children's relationships with caregivers: Mothers and child care teachers. *Child Development* 63: 859–78.

Howes, C., C.E. Hamilton, and L.C. Philipsen. 1998. Stability and continuity of child–caregiver and child–peer relationships. *Child Development* 69, no. 2: 418–26.

Howes, C., C.C. Matheson, and C.E. Hamilton. 1997. Maternal, teacher and child care history correlates of children's relationships with peers. *Child Development* 55: 257–73.

Howes, C., and S. Ritchie. 2002. *A matter of trust: Connecting teachers and learners in the early childhood classroom.* New York: Teachers College Press.

Kraft-Sayre, M.E., and R.C. Pianta. 2000. *Enhancing the transition to kindergarten: Linking children, families, and schools.* Charlottesville: University of Virginia, National Center for Early Development and Learning.

Kontos, S., and A. Wilcox-Herzog. 1997. Teachers' interactions with children: Why are they so important? *Young Children* 52, no. 2: 4–12.

Lally, J.R. 1995. The impact of child care policies and practices on infant/toddler identity formation. *Young Children* 51, no. 1: 58–67.

Margetts, K. 2002. Transition to school: Complexity and diversity. *European Early Childhood Education Research Journal* 10, no. 20: 103–14.

Nelson, F., and L. Garduque. 1991. The experience and perception of continuity between home and day care from the perspectives of child, mother, and caregiver. *Early Child Development and Care* 68: 99–111.

Peters, S. 2010. *Literature review: Transition from early childhood education to school.* http://www.educationcounts.govt.nz/publications/ece/literature-review-transition-from-early-childhood-education-to-school/executive-summary.

Pianta, R.C. 1996. The Student–Teacher Relationship Scale. University of Virginia, Charlottesville, VA. Unpublished.

Pianta, R.C. 1997. Adult–child relationship processes and early schooling. *Early Education and Development* 8, no. 1: 11–26.

Pianta, R.C., M.J. Cox, L. Taylor, and D. Early. 1999. Kindergarten teachers' practices related to the transition to school: Results of a national survey. *Elementary School Journal* 100, no. 1: 71–86.

Pianta, R.C., and M. Steinberg. 1992. Teacher–child relationships and adjusting to school. In *Beyond the parent: The role of other adults in children's lives*, ed. R.C. Pianta, 51–80. New Directions for Child Development: No. 57. San Francisco: Jossey-Bass.

Raikes, H. 1993. Relationship duration in infant care: Time with a high-ability teacher and infant–teacher attachment. *Early Childhood Research Quarterly* 8: 309–25.

Raikes, H. 1996. A secure base for babies: Applying attachment concepts to the infant care setting. *Young Children* 51, no. 5: 59–67.

Recchia, S.L., and K. Dvorakova. 2012. How three young toddlers transition from an infant to a toddler child care classroom: Exploring the influence of peer relationships, teacher expectations, and changing social contexts. *Early Education and Development* 23, no. 2: 181–201.

Recchia, S.L., and E. Loizou. 2002. Becoming an infant caregiver: Three profiles of personal and professional growth. *Journal of Research in Childhood Education* 16, no. 2: 133–47.

Recchia, S.L., and M. Shin. 2010. 'Baby teachers': How pre-service early childhood students transform their conceptions of teaching and learning through an infant practicum. *Early Years: An International Journal of Research and Development* 30, no. 2: 135–45.

Recchia, S.L., Y. Sekino, C. Brady-Smith, and A. Smedley. 2000, July. The development of infant–caregiver relationships in child care: Group patterns and individual differences. Poster presented at the XXIIth International Conference on Infant Studies, Brighton, UK.

Sander, L.W. 2000. Where are we going in the field of infant mental health? *Infant Mental Health Journal* 21, no. 1–2: 5–20.

Seifer, R., and M. Schiller. 1995. The role of parenting sensitivity, infant temperament, and dyadic interaction in attachment theory and assessment. In *Caregiving, cultural, and cognitive perspectives on secure-base behavior and working models: New growing points of attachment theory and research*, ed. E. Waters, B. Vaughn, G. Posada, and K. Kondo-Ikemura. Monographs of the Society for Research in Child Development, 60, no. 2–3): Series No. 244.

Sroufe, L.A. 1983. Infant–caregiver attachment and patterns of adaptation in preschool: The roots of maladaptation and competence. In *The Minnesota Symposium on Child Psychology*, Vol. 16, ed. M. Perlmutter. Hillsdale, NJ: Erlbaum.

Stake, R.E. 2005. Qualitative case studies. In *Handbook of qualitative research*, 3rd ed., ed. N.K. Denzin and Y.S. Lincoln, 443–66. Thousand Oaks, CA: Sage Publications.

Thompson, R.A. 2000. The legacy of early attachments. *Child Development* 71, no. 1: 145–52.

Waters, E. 1987. *Attachment Behavior Q-Set*, Revision 3.0. Unpublished instrument, State University of New York at Stony Brook, Department of Psychology.

Wolcott, H.F. 1994. *Transforming qualitative data: Description, analysis, and interpretation.* Thousand Oaks, CA: Sage Publications.

Documentation and analysis of children's experience: an ongoing collegial activity for early childhood professionals

Mariacristina Picchio[a], Donatella Giovannini[b], Susanna Mayer[a] and Tullia Musatti[a]

[a]Institute of Cognitive Sciences and Technologies, National Research Council of Italy, Rome, Italy; [b]Department of Education, City of Pistoia, Italy

Systematic documentation and analysis of educational practice can be a powerful tool for continuous support to the professionalism of early childhood education practitioners. This paper discusses data from a three-year action-research initiative carried out by a research agency in collaboration with a network of Italian municipal *nido* services. The action research aimed at elaborating and implementing documentation procedures that *nido* practitioners could accomplish continuously and that could form the basis of a collegial reflection on children's experience and the improvement of practices. The analysis of practitioners' discussions about weaknesses and strengths of the new procedures shows how they could be inscribed within the framework of their current professional engagement and support their processes of reflexivity. The analysis also highlights the important role of collegiality in sustaining practitioners' analysis, evaluation and improvement of their practice.

Introduction

Continuous professional support of practitioners in early childhood education is acknowledged to be an essential component of service quality by experts (Children in Europe 2008; NAEYC 1993; OECD 2001, 2006) as well as in political statements (European Commission Communication 2011; Europe de l'Enfance 2010).

Italian best practices in early childhood education, such as in Bologna, Parma, Pistoia and Reggio Emilia, have actually been accompanied by substantial investment in practitioners' professionalism. Most of the high-quality services are found within municipal ECE provision (Oberhuemer, Schreyer, and Neuman 2010) where continuous support to professionalism has been ensured by an insightful use of an amount of paid hours to be spent by practitioners in team meetings and in-service training (Musatti and Picchio 2010) and the activity of pedagogic coordinators (also named *pedagogista*), who support practitioners in their professional practice, organise in-service training initiatives, ensure interactions among services in the same area, and constitute a professional and organisational interface between services and the municipal administration (Musatti and Mayer 2003).

A number of elements characterise the approach to professionalism in Italian ECE best practices. Care and education activities are considered two inextricable dimensions of professional practice (Cameron and Moss 2007; Contini and Manini 2007) that should be aimed at guaranteeing children's learning as well as psychological and physical well-being. This perspective has entailed greater attention being paid to children's global experience in all its social, emotional and cognitive components, as it is displayed during their everyday life in the service. It is not surprising that practitioners working in Italian *nido* (service for under three-year-old children) have been defined as experts in young children's everyday life (Bondioli and Mantovani 1987).

Professionalism is coherently conceived as the acquisition of a reflective stance by practitioners (Dewey 1933) rather than the ability to implement pedagogic strategies and procedures. Practitioners' reflection remains strongly focused on educational practice through the habit of observing and documenting children's developmental changes, specific experiences or special events in the service. Through documentation, these ephemeral phenomena are recorded and become visible and can be subjected to later investigation and reflection aimed at the innovation of practices (Rinaldi 2005). Thus, most in-service training initiatives have been oriented towards exercising reflexivity through the analysis of practice based on documentation.

Last but not least, most Italian best practices in early childhood education are inspired by a participatory approach (Urban 2008), which stresses the importance of parental involvement and the sharing of educational choices between parents and practitioners (Rayna, Rubio, and Scheu 2010) while placing great emphasis on collegiality as a basic dimension of professionalism in education. The team provides both emotional and professional support. Communication and cooperation among practitioners are based on the opportunity to share the responsibility for the same group of children by working together for some hours a day. They are also nourished by team meetings and centre-based in-service training initiatives. Thus, collegiality also implies practitioners sharing reflection in order to plan activities with children or parents, prepare play materials and analyse the methodological or theoretical implications of their practice.

The continuous support to practitioners' professionalism has been a major ingredient of the ECE municipal provision in Pistoia, whose high quality is widely recognised (Musatti and Mayer 2001; Musatti, Picchio, and Mayer forthcoming). This support was realised through a coherent educational project in the city, a dynamic coordination team, carefully planned organisation of in-service training and other team and network meetings, the promotion of practitioners' use of observation and documentation practices, and collaboration with research agencies in Italy, Europe and the USA (Becchi 2010; Galardini 2009; Galardini and Giovannini 2001). However, also in Pistoia, in the last decade, a substantial number of expert ECE practitioners retired and were replaced by young practitioners with a different cultural and educational background. Thus, the management of the municipal ECE sector took action to maintain continuity of the educational culture of the city across generations of practitioners. In 2006, the director of the municipal education board in Pistoia invited the National Research Council of Italy (ISTC-CNR), with which it had had a long-lasting cooperation, to carry out an action-research initiative in collaboration with the network of municipal *nido* services in order to develop new documentation procedures that practitioners could accomplish continuously and that could form the basis of collegial reflection on children's experience and on practice improvement.

Theoretical frame

Planning and implementing the action research raised some major theoretical questions. A first set of questions concerns how to document the children's experience during their everyday life in the *nido*. This means capturing and describing the phenomena embodying the uniqueness of the events, the complex relations among them, and the children's resulting experience. As the flow of everyday life in an early childhood educational setting is characterised by a particular tension between continuity and change, expressing the process dimension of children's experience presents a further challenge. Thus, documenting children's everyday experience requires several distinct but interrelated abilities, such as to observe a variety of contemporary and successive phenomena, reconstruct their meanings and relations, and organise all this into a synthetic narrative.

Practitioners, as reflective participants in the experience taking place in the setting, are the best candidates for describing it in its basic social and cognitive components without losing sight of its core meaning. Nevertheless, in order to produce a narrative of the experience in which they have participated, they have to be able to distance themselves from it.

According to Schön (1983) the temporal distance from practice is highly relevant in determining the nature and effect of practitioners' reflection. The author has pointed out that the time-span during which the practitioner's action has an effect, i.e. what he defined as the *action-present*, delimits also the boundary beyond which reflection-*in*-action, when the practitioner thinks about doing something while doing it, will become reflection-*on*-action, when she/he analyses what she/he did or what happened.

In contrast with Schön's view, Perrenoud (2001) has argued that in educational practice the different levels of reflection are marked by the extension of its object – a single action or set of similar actions – rather than by the temporal distance from practice.

In early childhood practitioners' reflection, the temporal distance from practice necessarily implies different levels of reflection. The flow of children's experience can be segmented into temporal units that are significant with reference to different developmental processes. Consequently, changes in children's experience and the impact of practitioners' actions on it can be highlighted quite differently according to the temporal unit considered. Thus, for early childhood education practitioners the transition from reflection-*in*-action, when they are concerned with the immediate impact of their educational action, to reflection-*on*-action, when they can evaluate the achievement of educational goals and objectives, is largely determined by the extension of the temporal unit considered. Documentation procedures should be devised accordingly.

Another set of questions concerns the relationships between documentation activity and the collegial dimension of reflection. Sharing reflection with others contributes to blurring the boundaries between reflection-*in*-action and their reflection-*on*-action. Sharing reflection-*in*-action, that is a coherent coordination of practitioners' actions, is based on their individual acquisition of common habits in implementing their practice, but it is achieved only by making explicit to each other experiences and thoughts outside the action context. On the other hand, sharing reflection-*on*-action enhances psychological distancing from practice but is nourished by a consciously shared experience during practice. Also in this case, reflecting and discussing among colleagues makes for clearer judgements and a better agreement concerning educational goals and objectives. Documentation procedures should support these processes of sharing reflection among practitioners.

This study

On the basis of the above considerations a set of documentation procedures was developed. The participation of Pistoia *nido* practitioners was crucial in both devising and trying out the new procedures. Their reflections and comments during the research meetings made visible the progression of the action research as well as their increasingly insightful competence in observing and analysing children's experience (Reason 2006). This article will present an analysis of the practitioners' voices.

Participants and methods

A research group was set up, comprising the pedagogic coordinators in Pistoia, seven *nido* practitioners (called teachers in Pistoia), and five researchers from the research agency. A cascading procedure, which was inscribed within a framework of in-service training, provided the involvement of all the Pistoia *nido* practitioners in the action research. The research group met periodically and elaborated the documentation procedures, which were then proposed, tested and discussed by all the teachers during *nido* or inter-*nido* meetings. These discussions were reported in the research group meetings for further elaborations which were, then, presented to the whole group of *nido* teachers at the end of every educational year. The initiative lasted three educational years (2006–2009), during which numerous meetings were held periodically. Two years later, two further research group meetings were held in order to take stock of the evolution of the experience.

All the discussions made during the research group meetings (n = 11) and the general meetings (n = 3) were recorded and entirely transcribed.

In the following, we present the documentation procedures used and analyse the teachers' discussions regarding the difficulties and benefits of their use.

Findings

Weekly Reports

The first documentation derived from a previous study (Musatti and Mayer 2011) following which Pistoia *nido* practitioners acquired the habit of writing notes on children's everyday life during their week in the *nido*. In the new project, the utilisation of these notes for reflection on practice was discussed.

First, it was decided that the notes written by teachers each week would be transformed into a more coherent narrative of children's experience in the *nido*. The teachers confirmed that the week was a significant temporal unit of the children's experience in the *nido* and that writing was the best means for expressing a narrative. The Weekly Report would consist of a one- to three-page-long written narrative that should be organised according to a guideline that listed the principal dimensions of the children's daily experience in the *nido*: children's home-*nido*-home daily transition; the social processes among children and between children and adults; children's play or exploration; children's behaviour during care activities; children's use of the spatial setting; the temporal dimension of children's experience during the day.[1] The teachers had to keep in mind the guideline in observing children's experience, consider the entire flow of events during the week, try to capture the common ground of the successive events, and, ultimately, analyse what these events meant in children's experience.

At the end of the week (mostly on Friday afternoon, during the children's naptime), the team of *nido* teachers in charge of each group of children met and discussed the content of the report that was then written together or by one of them. When the procedure was well established, most of the *nido* teams decided to publish a copy of their Weekly Report in order to inform the parents of the children's experience.

The benefits and difficulties of the Weekly Reports were extensively and repeatedly discussed.

Capturing and narrating children's global experience

The first difficulty was to acknowledge that the variety of interactions among children's and adults' activities, social behaviours and locations in the setting all come to constitute the experience offered to children as a meaningful whole. This global meaning had to be captured and narrated. This meant that teachers needed to focus their attention on significant elements underlying the flow of everyday life in the *nido* rather than on the behaviour of individual children or on specific moments of everyday life. They then had to link these elements together to form a clear and coherent narrative rather than to give a mere account of the events:

> A: The greatest difficulty for many of us is how to grasp the overall picture as it is very easy to dwell on one episode and lose sight of the overall picture. (18.01.2007)

> D: The first Weekly Reports were very long. We would write: 'On Monday, such and such happened, on Tuesday, such and such'. We soon realized that this was not the right way to capture the essence of what happened over a week of daily life spent with the children. (3.03.2009)

The teachers acknowledged that the guideline helped them to consider the various aspects of the educational setting even when they were taking part in it:

> C: [The guideline] makes us observe in a different way. There is a big difference between having a guide and not having one when we observe children. Before this I used to make notes on the children's activities but it was just observing for the sake of observing. (17.02.2009)

The impact on educational action

The Weekly Report retains the perspective of an actor who participated actively in the daily life setting described. The report writer must be in a position to view her/himself as one of the subjects involved and at the same time view her/himself from the outside. This process, although perceived as requiring considerable effort, gave the teachers greater awareness also of their own way of participating in the educational situation. The following excerpts highlight how documenting a full week facilitates distancing oneself from the experience and, at the same time, supports the transition from reflection-*in*-action to reflection-*on*-action:

A: The Weekly Report also teaches us to understand what we experienced in the educational context better, because retracing what happened at the end of the week entails having to go back into the situation while keeping a distant stance. (17.02.2009)

R: In my view, this reflection that we perform at the end of a week's work with the children, in which we are involved as actors, leads us to review step by step what we have done…. We must make an effort, but it is an effort that enables us to approach a situation from a different angle, in a more conscious and reflective way. (17.02.2009)

Writing the Weekly Report also turned out to be a sustainable commitment for the teachers because it provided them with an immediate benefit. As some teachers clearly expressed in the following excerpts, the Weekly Report can restore significance and value to their work and relieve them of the strain that arises out of the sensation of being squeezed by the flow of daily life with children:

G: Sometimes you wonder 'what is it that I have done, where am I at?'. There is a moment of disarray when you feel you have not done anything, and yet many things have actually happened. (17.02.2009)

D: The Weekly Report enables you to observe yourself from a distance, to observe with some detachment what you have done, it immediately made you feel somehow relieved of a load…. The load due to the feeling of being cancelled out through the daily routine with the children, because you are caught up inside that constant, unceasing flow of things to do, of moments to experience, of sensations and emotions. (3.03.2009)

As emerges from the following excerpts, the teachers confirm that the concise, constant and systematic documentation of the children's experience during the week helps to focus on the aspects of continuity and change occurring within it, to grasp more fully the ongoing processes and to redirect one's educational practice with greater awareness:

S: Since I began documenting in the Weekly Report all the proposals made to the children, I managed to synthesize them more satisfactorily and to link them together. Therefore, day by day, I managed to create this thread that then links them all together. (17.02.2009)

M: Over time many details emerge, many small facets, a lot of fleeting moments, that nevertheless allow the activity to progress, that enable you to develop a way of viewing how the whole day progresses … I can now appreciate how things evolve. (17.02.2009)

G: Preparing the Weekly Report puts me precisely in the position of understanding what has happened, linking together the events and the situations, thus enabling me to say 'I can start from here'. (17.02.2009)

Joint reflection

The systematic opportunity to devote some time at the end of each week to swap opinions on what happened strengthens the collegial dimension of the educational work, as is shown by the following excerpts:

Do: The nicest aspect was the discussion among colleagues that emerged from the reading of the reports when what had been written was debated, why it had been written and what its significance was. (18.01.2007)

D: Opportunities for sharing reflection were always available to the *nido* team, but writing the Weekly Report obliged us to engage in a different kind of reflection, more focused, moment by moment – we were compelled to come to an agreement. It was not simply a matter of meeting together and describing one's perceptions, one's point of view, but rather of coming to an agreement. On the same event, each one would make her own observation but what was ultimately written down was something shared and therefore had an extremely important value for us…. We realized that the benefits consisted not only in preparing documentation but in feeling that our educational practice was more consolidated. Our choices were no longer left to chance, unsupported by reflection, but were carefully weighed as they were shared. (3.03.2009)

Two years later, the teachers confirmed their intention to go on writing the Weekly Reports and again pointed out how they represent a shared memory of the experience made and support their shared reflection on future actions:

M: I have always viewed the Weekly Report also as an opportunity for sharing among teachers that would also help us to develop, as a training opportunity. (11.05.2011)

S: We find it very satisfying that now all three of us write the Weekly Report. The year I was left alone to do it was terribly frustrating as I was not able to share with anyone, and I started to lose track of the weeks. (11.05.2011)

Documenting an extended period of experience – Process Reports

As we have shown, the teachers expressed overall agreement on the utility of writing the Weekly Reports to document the development of children's experience during each week, as well as the links between one week and the next. Nevertheless, everyone agreed that in order to direct educational practice it is also necessary to grasp the processes that take place over a longer period of time. Thus, it was decided to produce another written report that would consider children's experience over half of the educational year, as this was considered a meaningful segment of children's life in the *nido*. This Process Report, as it was named, was based on the sequential analysis of the Weekly Reports written during this period. It was aimed to capture the elements of continuity or change emerging from the analysis and to express the 'essence' of the development of the children's experience.

Writing this report presented a further challenge to the teachers' competences in capturing and narrating the meaningful aspects of the processes of children's experience.

A comparative analysis of the Weekly Reports may reveal meaningful aspects of the children's experience that had escaped the teachers' attention when they were analysed from week to week, as emerges from the following excerpts:

D: I think that the Process Report is a good tool to master what is happening, because in the Weekly Report we can skip something important. When we have to reconstruct five months we become aware of a lot of things. (16.05.2008)

G: We re-read the Weekly Reports together and highlighted the important points, interrogating each other as to the choices made and discussing them. This work showed us the point we had reached. Up to now we had the impression of having worked, of having done many things, without grasping the core of the question. [For example] we were able to understand more what the group of children were interested in during this period. (18.01.2007)

Evaluating the development of children's experience

It was immediately evident that considering a more extended temporal unit leads to a higher level of reflection on the development of children's experience. Describing its more significant processes and then discussing them – 'interrogating the Process Report' to use the participants' words – ultimately means to assess whether they are moving in the direction of the educational objectives pursued. Thus, the research group spent a considerable amount of time defining the educational objectives that could serve as a frame of reference for evaluating the processes described in the Process Report.

The Pistoia teachers already shared a basic educational project that consisted of goals and objectives to be pursued rather than a package of practices and actions to be implemented. However, it was acknowledged that they had to make explicit the specific educational objectives – in relation to children's development and the evolution of their experience in the *nido* (sociality, familiarity with the setting, autonomy, engagement, etc.), to be pursued in daily practice with each children's age group over the period considered in the report. These objectives should of course be consistent with the educational project of the Pistoia ECE provision and be further adapted by each group of teachers to suit the characteristics of the specific group of children with whom they worked each year. The following excerpts illustrate this dual perspective:

> Do: The main effort was to detail specific objectives that were inherent in our educational practice…. It was a way of restating more precisely the vision, image and overall philosophy of Pistoia *nido*. (8.09.2007)

> C: At the beginning of the year it is absolutely essential to set these explicit objectives before starting out. Each teacher will then fit them into the context of their own group of children. (26.02.2007)

As shown by the following excerpts, analysis of the Process Report in relation to the objectives can re-orient the educational practice in many ways.

It can highlight any critical points in the educational context:

> An: We drew up the Process Report to describe what had happened during the four months in question and then we tried to evaluate the type of work, the pathway followed, the resulting history, in relation to the objectives. At this point we became aware of the difficulties, of the critical factors. (12.02.2008)

It supports the long-term planning of educational activities:

> V: This procedure supports reflection on the path to be followed … obliges us to order our ideas, intentions. At the beginning of the year you meet with your colleagues and say: 'From now to January…'. (12.02.2008)

Actually, the drafting of the Process Report and its evaluation are closely linked. Raising the question of whether an objective has been attained leads the teachers to tackle issues that they have unwittingly neglected, as emerges from the following interaction:

> Do: What benefit did you obtain from interrogating the Process Report? For instance, with reference to the development of sociality in the *nido* what did it tell you?

D replies: First of all, I became aware of the shortcomings. For example, when I analysed the Weekly Reports I found no trace of the interactions between me, the adult, and the children. In my opinion, this is something positive. This is important, don't you think? To see that I was not in a position to answer that question. Did I not know or had I just not documented it? (11.02.2008)

On the other hand, the Process Report provides evidence on which teachers can base their evaluations:

Do: When I analyse the Process Report, I can see whether the effects of the educational practice are consistent with the objectives. However, I must not just say whether we reached an objective. I must explain my judgement on the basis of what I have described. (16.05.2008)

Sharing the evaluation

The evaluation of children's experience, as it is described in the Process Report, implies reflecting at a higher level. Teachers point out that sharing it with colleagues who did not participate in the educational context analysed can support this further removed from practice reflection:

C: Different questions emerge according to whether the Process Report is discussed in the *nido* meeting or in the inter-*nido* meeting, when we meet colleagues not involved in the situation described. In the *nido* meeting, we are persons who are involved in the same situation. We take for granted some issues that should be made explicit. (18.01.2007)

R: Whether the objective has been attained must be sorted out in the team discussion of the Process Report, not among the teachers of the same group. (11.02.2008)

A: Analysis of the Process Report and the evaluation of the path followed is meaningful only if we share them with other colleagues. Otherwise, I am simply asking a question and providing my own answers. As soon as I interact with others it truly becomes an opportunity to understand the problems. (16.05.2008)

Difficulties in writing and evaluating the Process Report

Despite the teachers' commitment and enthusiasm in formulating detailed educational objectives and their general appreciation of a procedure of periodic assessment of the educational context, the writing and analysis of the Process Report did not become a professional habit for the *nido* teachers at Pistoia.

We identified a number of major difficulties encountered by the teachers. The extra effort required to express concisely in writing the 'essence' of children's experience over a period of four–five months clashed with the teachers' still uncertain mastery in producing a written narrative. More importantly, keeping separate the description and analysis of the processes from their evaluation was not easy. As we have shown, the heightened awareness of the educational objectives guided the teachers in their efforts to identify the developmental processes occurring in the children's experience. However, the focus on the objectives often led the teachers to dwell on the evaluation of what they could observe at the time of writing the Process Report and to neglect the documentation and analysis of the processes taking place during the whole period considered.

Furthermore, the teachers seemed to find it particularly difficult to reflect at the higher level of abstraction required by the analysis of an extended period of children's experience and to use this reflection for redirecting their educational action. In the verification meetings held after two years it was above all these difficulties that were discussed:

D: That is the hardest part, keeping track of a pathway lasting so many months. (11.05.2011)

C: When you get to produce the Process Report in January/February, September is now in the distant past. If something needs to be changed it is now too late. (11.05.2011)

Concluding remarks

The analysis of the practitioners' discussions of the documentation procedures proposed during the action research has shown that the systematic documentation, analysis and evaluation of educational practice can be a powerful tool of continuous support to the professionalism of early childhood education practitioners. In particular, it has highlighted the important role of collegiality in sustaining practitioners' processes of reflexivity and, consequently, the need for documentation procedures that will support processes of sharing among practitioners.

The choice of written documentation was found to be appropriate. Writing sustains the narrative elaboration of what has been observed in daily practice, constitutes a material reference for group discussion and remains as a memory of shared reflection. Although practitioners may not be familiar with writing, it remains an available means of documentation in most contexts.

In order to document, analyse and evaluate the children's experience in the *nido*, stable procedures are needed that can be easily integrated into everyday professional practice. Pistoia *nido* practitioners readily accepted the documentation procedures proposed, as they were already accustomed to documentation and collegial reflection. The new documentation procedures, which aimed to accompany the development of children's experience in the *nido* and make visible its processes and significance, provided a more stable framework for exercising and sharing reflexivity.

However, it must be stressed that the documentation procedures could play this role to the extent that they were the result of a shared engagement, they could accompany the development of the shared reflection without overwhelming it, and they could be used for the shared planning of educational practice.

The procedures for writing and analysing the Weekly Report were easily inscribed within the professional practice of Pistoia *nido* practitioners, as their rhythm was found to be compatible with the practitioners' work organisation. More importantly, these procedures reinforced collegiality as they provided the opportunity for practitioners to meet and share information, judgements and intents, according to rhythms and modalities that had an immediate and fruitful impact on the educational action.

The procedures for writing and questioning the Process Report were found to be less easily sustained and, at the reappraisal carried out two years later, the research group discussed their revision. As our analysis has shown, both the greater temporal distance and the higher level of abstraction involved in writing and questioning the Process Report induced a reflection-*on*-action, the impact of which on practice could not be immediately perceived by the practitioners. It is noteworthy that sharing reflexivity processes with other colleagues emerged as the best source of support in coping with this difficulty.

Acknowledgements

This article analyses data from the action-research project 'The quality of children's experience in the *nido*' conducted in collaboration by the Institute of Cognitive Sciences and Technologies, National Research Council of Italy and the Department of Education of the City of Pistoia, Italy. The authors wish to thank all the other participants in the project, for Pistoia: Rita Benedetto, Deborak Cappellini, Rossella Chietti, Annalia Fragai, Armanda Cassaresi, Franca Gualtieri, Gabri Magrini, Valentina Magni, Cristina Mariotti, Silvana Stroppa, Monica Tonini; for ISTC-CNR: Isabella Di Giandomenico and Patrizia Sposetti, as well as all the Pistoia *nido* practitioners. Special and warm thanks go to Anna Lia Galardini and Sonia Iozzelli, former Head of the Department of Education of the City of Pistoia, for offering the authors the opportunity to conduct the research-action study.

Note

1. The guidelines are extensively illustrated in Di Giandomenico, Musatti, and Picchio (2011).

References

Becchi, E. 2010. *Una pedagogia del buon gusto. Esperienze e progetti nei servizi educativi per l'infanzia del Comune di Pistoia.* [Pedagogy of 'good taste'. Experiences and projects in Pistoia municipal ECE services]. Milan: FrancoAngeli.

Bondioli, A., and S. Mantovani, eds. 1987. *Manuale critico dell'asilo nido.* [Critical Handbook of *Nido*]. Milan: FrancoAngeli.

Cameron, C., and P. Moss. 2007. *Care Work in Europe. Current understandings and future directions.* London: Routledge.

Children in Europe Policy. 2008. Young children and their services: Developing a European approach. *Children in Europe*, September.

Contini, M., and M. Manini, eds. 2007. *La cura in educazione* [Care in education]. Rome: Carocci.

Dewey, J. 1933. *How we think? A reassessment of the relation of reflective thinking in the educational processes.* Chicago: Henry Regnery.

Di Giandomenico, I., T. Musatti, and M. Picchio. 2011. Using written reports as a tool for analysis and evaluation of children's experience in day care centre. In *ERATO – Analyse, evaluate and innovate: A guide for early childhood education and care (0–6)*, ed. EADAP, 70–90. Edinburgh: Children in Scotland.

European Commission Communication. 2011. *Early childhood education and care: Providing all our children with the best start for the world of tomorrow.* (COM(2011)66).

Europe de l'Enfance 2010. Declaration of the Permanent Intergovernmental Group 'Europe de l'Enfance', Meeting on November 16, 2010, Brussels. http://www.childoneurope.org/ee/pdf/Declaration_REME%20_Eng_version_25_11_2010.pdf.

Galardini, A.L. 2009. Réseau et documentation: l'expérience italienne pour la qualité éducative. In *Pour un accueil de qualité de la petite enfance. quel curriculum?*, ed. S. Rayna, C. Bouve and P. Moisset, 79–86. Toulouse: Édition Érès.

Galardini, A.L., and D. Giovannini. 2001. Pistoia: Creating a dynamic, open system to serve children, families and community. In *Bambini· The Italian spproach to infant/toddler care*, ed. L. Gandini and C. Pope Edwards, 89–104. New York: Teachers College Press.

Musatti, T., and S. Mayer. 2001. Knowing and learning in an educational context: A study in the Infant-Toddler Centers of the City of Pistoia. In *Bambini: The Italian Approach to Infant/Toddler Care*, ed. L. Gandini and C. Pope Edwards, 167–80. New York: Teachers College Press.

Musatti, T., and S. Mayer, eds. 2003. *Il coordinamento dei servizi educativi per l'infanzia. Una funzione emergente in Italia e in Europa.* [The coordination of ECE services. An emerging function in Italy and Europe]. Azzano San Paolo, BG: Edizioni Junior.

Musatti, T., and S. Mayer. 2011. Sharing attention and activities among toddlers: The spatial dimension of the setting and the educator's role. *European Early Childhood Research Journal* 19, no. 2: 207–21.

Musatti, T., and M. Picchio. 2010. Early education in Italy: Research and practice. *International Journal of Early Childhood* 42: 141–53.

Musatti, T., M. Picchio, and S. Mayer. Forthcoming. A continuous support to professionalism: The case of Pistoia ECE provision. In *CoRe: Competence Requirement in Early Childhood Education and Care. A study for the European Commission Directorate General for Education and Culture*, ed. M. Urban, M. Vandenbroeck, J. Peeters, K. Van Laere and A. Lazzari, Brussels: European Commission.

NAEYC. 1993. *A conceptual framework for early childhood professional development.* Washington, DC: National Association for the Education of Young Children.

Oberhuemer, P., I. Schreyer, and M.J. Neuman. 2010. *Professionals in early childhood education and care systems.* Opladen & Farmington Hills, MI: Barbara Budrich.

OECD. 2001. *Starting strong: Early childhood education and care.* Paris: Organisation for Economic Co-operation and Development.

OECD. 2006. *Starting strong II: Early childhood education and care.* Paris: Organisation for Economic Co-operation and Development.

Perrenoud, P. 2001. *Développer la pratique réflexive dans le métier d'enseignant.* Paris: ESF.

Rayna, S., M.M. Rubio, and H. Scheu. 2010. *Parents-professionnels: la coéducation en questions.* Toulouse: Editions Érès.

Reason, P. 2006. Choice and quality in action research practice. *Journal of Management Inquiry* 15, no. 2: 187–203.

Rinaldi, C. 2005. *In dialogue with Reggio Emilia.* New York: Routledge.

Schön, D.A. 1983. *The reflective practitioner.* New York: Basic Books.

Urban, M. 2008. Dealing with uncertainty: Challenges and possibilities for the early childhood profession. *European Early Childhood Research Journal* 16, no. 2: 135–52.

Accompaniment and quality in childcare services: the emergence of a culture of professionalization

Florence Pirard[a] and Jean-Marie Barbier[b]

[a]Department of Education and Training, University of Liège, Liège, Belgium; [b]Centre de recherche sur la formation (CRF), Conservatoire des Arts et Métiers (CNAM), Paris, France

This article addresses various educational cultures observed today in a variety of training and professional development contexts in the field of early childhood education. The paper also analyses methods of developing and implementing training or professional 'accompaniment'. This notion of 'accompaniment' has been developed in the context of French-speaking countries, especially in relation to the development of childcare services and the search for quality. From a case study using 'accompaniment' as a professional development initiative to consider freedom of movement for children aged birth to three years as a quality criterion in daily educational practice, the article illustrates the importance of considering innovation in the professional development of early years educators, not only as a new initiative in this specific context, but also as a signifier of the wider emergence of a new culture of professionalization where actions, actors and environment undergo change simultaneously.

Introduction

Improving the quality of childcare services for children under three years of age remains a challenge in many European countries where the structure of service supply is divided and where the qualifications and professional training opportunities available often fail to reach agreed professional standards (OECD 2006; EACEA 2009; Penn 2009; Bennett 2010; Pirard 2011b). The challenge consists not only in improving the standard of qualifications (European Commission Childcare Network 1996; Children in Europe 2008; UNICEF 2008; Leseman 2009), but also in creating a new emphasis: a more holistic approach, where the social, economic and psycho-educational dimensions of childcare services are included (Vandenbroeck, Pirard and Peeters, 2009). This would be a more open approach, where predefined knowledge is considered an important base to co-construct new action-knowledge, as well as other educational practices, in situ while taking into account the points of view of other professionals, children, families and communities (Oberhuemer 2005; Pirard 2011b).

This open approach would generate the development of new functions of professional 'accompaniment', a term very often referred to in French literature (Paul 2005; Pirard 2007; Beauvais 2008; Barbier in press), but very difficult to translate into English. Often associated with 'coaching', 'mentoring' and 'counselling' functions, without being substituted by these concepts, accompaniment considers the process in which the activity of one person (the accompanier) is combined with the activity of another (the accompanied practitioner) in order not only to develop the professional competencies of both, but also to transform the daily educational practice (i.e. the 'systemic competencies', Urban et al. 2011). Three main characteristics of the accompaniment can be identified in the French literature. First, accompaniment is a continuous, interactive and open process that can produce certain unforeseen outcomes. Second, the accompanier is seen as a resource person and the accompanied practitioner as an individual or collective actor working either in the same activity domain or without any specialization. Finally, accompaniment aims to develop some individual and systemic competencies in situ. The competencies result from the holistic process of accompaniment and are more than professional knowledge transmitted through teaching, or skills acquired during training sessions.

These trends hide the fact that there are many ways of interpreting and operating training systems and organizations nowadays. Oberhuemer, Schreyer and Neuman refer to 'cultural scripts':

> ... research located within diverse theoretical frameworks – e.g. comparative education studies, the social history and sociology of childhood, cultural psychology – suggests that our images of childhood, learning, and development are initially constructed within specific historical, cultural, economic and geo-political contexts.... These 'cultural scripts' (Rosenthal 2003) not only permeate our conceptions of early childhood centres as a public good, but also our images of those who work with young children. (2010, 480)

So these 'cultural scripts' may permeate our images of the education and training of childcare workers.

Nowadays there is a consensus on recognizing the value of a diversity of approaches, and on highlighting the risks incurred by the standardization of training systems (Cameron and Moss 2007; Peeters 2008; Urban 2008; Bennett 2010; Oberhuemer, Schreyer, and Neuman 2010). However, this approach necessitates a public debate: 'every interpretation of professionalism must be continually questioned and made transparent through dialogue and debate' (Peeters 2008, 58). This article will offer some practical and theoretical references to illustrate the diversity of training and education practice, and on this basis debate training systems and questions of professionalization in the field of early childhood education.

From the notion of 'accompaniment' to the emergence of a new educational action culture

The debate over teaching and training is also important in French-speaking countries, for example in France and Belgium. A review of the literature presents some results of reforms made in the training system, i.e. the 'educateurs jeunes enfants' in France (Peeters 2008; Urban et al. 2011) and some new directions for curriculum, teaching, training and the arrival of the new notion of 'accompaniment' (Rayna, Bouve, and Moisset 2009; Pirard 2011b).

The debate over teaching, training and 'accompaniment' is not limited to the practical question of how to prepare and 'accompany' professionals who work in childcare services, but also asks further theoretical questions. How do we currently view the relationship between service development and the evolution of training? What are our conceptions of training and adult education for professionals who work in childcare services? Which representations of educational approaches, of their practitioners and their relationships with the wider environment should we consider?

The question of training systems and their relationship to service development is particularly significant in the field of early childhood education, but should not be confined to this sector: French studies of professionalization in adult training and education can give some interesting insights to identify more general changes, and to interpret this evolution in a global perspective.

In the wider field of education and adult training, Barbier (2005, 2009) described three cultures of education and training that have successively appeared in the Western world: first the 'culture de l'enseignement' ('culture of teaching'), second the 'culture de la formation' ('culture of training') and finally, the 'culture de la professionnalisation' ('culture of professionalization') (see Table 1).

In the teaching culture ('culture de l'enseignement'), knowledge is a central reference for educational work, based on the hypothesis of the transformation of identity through the appropriation of predefined knowledge. The educational space can be seen as a specialized space where knowledge is to be transmitted to pupils by the teacher in a suitable way; this space creates a hierarchy headed by the person who holds and is able to transmit knowledge ('the teacher'). It conceptualizes the relationship between theory and practice as an application process; new knowledge or new subjects are seen as the primary driver of change. This teaching culture, the most common cultural framework in the field of education and training, views educational action as a communication process (through courses, didactic activities, educational programmes, e-learning, thematic seminars and so on).

In the training culture ('culture de la formation'), developed in parallel to the traditional educational model (and sometimes in opposition to it), ability or skill forms the central reference for educational work based on the hypothesis of the transformation of identity through a process of transfer of new skills. The educational space can be seen as a specialized and 'protected space' (Bourgeois 1996), where new skills and abilities can be acquired and then applied to other contexts and situations (for instance, the work context). This space creates a hierarchy headed by the person who organizes specific learning situations ('the trainer') and who conceptualizes the 'decontextualization–reconceptualization' process. New practice is seen as the primary driver of change. The training culture views educational action as a space and a time to transform abilities and skills (the educational space and time) which can then be transferred to other contexts (both the labour and social space/time). This culture is found predominantly in training programmes aiming for technical goals, but also in general skills training promoting empathy, listening skills, etc.

The dialectic relationship between these two educational cultures contributed to the emergence of a third culture in the 1990s: the culture of professionalization ('culture de la professionnalisation'), which considers the notion of competence as the central theme for educational work, based on the hypothesis that action and actors can be jointly and simultaneously transformed. The educational space can be seen as a space for developing competencies in context, in an evolutionary process of activity. This space gives a primary position to the person who 'accompanies'

Table 1. Educational action cultures.

	Teaching culture	Training culture	Professionalization culture
Core theme	Knowledge	Capacity/skill/abilities	Competence
Representation of space and time of educational work	Space of knowledge acquisition through an appropriate medium	Space of production of new capacities transferrable to other situations	Space of goods and/or services production organized as a space for competences development
Hypothesis on identity transformations based on educational work	Appropriation	Transfer	Joined transformation of actor and action
Symbolic device (figure)	Teacher, considered as the owner and knowledge transmitter	Trainer, considered as the organizer of learning situations	Accompanier of professional development
Representation of target audience	Student	Learner	Practitioner or operator
Representation of links with the environment	Conceptualization – application (theory and practice)	Decontextualization–recontextualization	Joint transformation of action and action environment
Representation of motivation for change	Appearance of new knowledge or new disciplines	Appearance of new practice or new practice fields	Appearance of management practice linked to operations previously disjoined

Source: Barbier (2005, 124).

the professional development of practitioners (the 'Reflective Practitioner', Schön 1983) and at the same time to the transformation of practice and of the environment. New combined practice (previously separated) is seen as the primary driver of change. The culture of professionalization views and organizes the space and time of services and products as a space and time where individual and collective competencies are developed. This culture is present in activities such as action-research, mentoring and 'accompaniment'.

Research has illustrated the way in which these three cultures coexist in early childhood education, and in care training action systems (Pirard 2007). Although many initiatives are founded on teaching and training cultures, we can also observe over the last few decades the development of initiatives founded on another culture, that of professionalization. Different methods are available to document, analyze and evaluate practice and its effects on children and families (Pirard 2011a). They aim at once to develop new competencies in practitioners and to improve the quality of services. People who are not trainers or teachers – for example coordinators of day-care services in a city (Baudelot and Rayna 2000; Baudelot, Mayer, Musatti and Rayna 2002; Musatti and Mayer 2003) or advisers in education at a regional level (Pirard 2011b) – develop actions that aim to jointly transform competencies (both their own and those of other practitioners) and daily educational practice, and to improve conditions within a local dynamic. This process can generate a global and systemic transformation process for those involved (children, families, practitioners, elected post-holders, the local community), with associated transformations of actions (social and educational practice) and of the local environment.

This evolution in educational culture can be connected with the evolution of approaches to addressing service quality (Pirard 2007). Arguably, a normative quality approach can be associated with a teaching culture; alternatively, an ecological, inclusive and effective quality approach (Moss, Dahlberg, and Pence 2002; Dahlberg and Moss 2005) could generate a new way of conceptualizing the training of professionals. The result would be professionals who are no longer seen as isolated technicians or experts in their specific field, but as members of communities able to develop a reflective, rather than simply reflexive approach (Peeters and Vandenbroeck 2011); to co-construct and regulate daily practice on the basis of shared observation, discussion and argumentation; and to participate in coeducation (Brougère 2010), in order to develop a democratic local forum in the childcare services. This evolution can be seen as the expression of the emergence of a new educational culture in childcare education: the culture of professionalization (Pirard 2007).

An accompaniment process case study

We will now present a case study based on the notion 'Freedom of movement for young children' to illustrate the importance of educational cultures in understanding the development of training theory and practice, and perspectives in the field of early childhood education. The case study is taken from a rural setting in the French Community of Belgium (in Luxembourg Province) from 2004 to 2009.

Before going further, it is important to mention that in the French Community, a new curriculum, 'Accueillir les tout petits, oser la qualité' ('Welcoming the early years; taking up the challenge of quality', 2002), was developed by means of a participatory process involving professionals taking care of children under three. This curriculum was implemented from 2002 by agents of the public institution (Office de la Naissance et de l'Enfance, ONE) in charge of authorizing, financing, evaluating and accompanying childcare services. These agents carry out their roles with reference to laws recently issued (especially the 'Code de Qualité de l'accueil', 1999, revised in 2003). ONE coordinators who accompany and evaluate childcare services (0–12 years) in a given district and advisers in education who accompany coordinators and practitioners of childcare services have played a major role in curriculum implementation. The chosen method of implementation seeks to reinforce professionalization while avoiding undesirable standardisation of outcomes (Pirard 2011b).

At the beginning of 2004, a coordinator from the Office de la Naissance et de l'Enfance (ONE),with responsibility for controlling, evaluating and 'accompanying' day care services in five districts, decided to try out the tools associated with the new curriculum in Luxembourg province. She asked the adviser responsible for developing education in the same province to co-observe the educational practice in one voluntary day-care service (0–3 years), as she intended to experiment with a new curriculum. Both coordinator and adviser had many criteria to observe, which were seen as reference points for considering childcare quality. One of these quality criteria concerned the notion of 'freedom of movement' based on Pikler's research (Pikler 2006), as follows:

> … the stages of psychomotor development are achieved through children's initiatives, without a 'teaching' intervention by the adult…. Freedom of movement consists in leaving children free in all their spontaneous corporal movements, unhindered and without teaching any movement whatsoever…. Control of their own motor development influences the development of the whole personality of these children and affects their mental development…. (Accueillir les tout-petits, oser la qualité [Welcoming the early years: taking up the challenge of quality] 2002, 104)

The curriculum also emphasises the importance of the choice of games, objects and space in the environment. These are the conditions that allow each child to explore and experiment with his/her competencies without any specific stimulus.

In Luxembourg Province, this criterion of freedom of movement for young children was almost unknown to the professionals in day-care services, where complicated materials, objects and games were made available to children who could therefore only do what the objects allowed them to do, precluding real experimentation. The practices observed there were at odds with the criteria used to evaluate service provision. The professionals were not familiar with questions such as: how to support babies, how to view babies' activity, how to accompany young children in their psychomotor development. The discovery of this gap between what is identified as an essential condition of childcare quality in the curriculum and what is done in practice led the 'accompaniers' to conceptualize, organize, analyse, evaluate and regulate different kinds of actions undertaken within a global perspective.

The gap between the criteria established in the 'reference framework' and the practice observed in situ is very common and could be addressed in a number of ways: through the organization of training sessions to communicate unknown knowledge (characteristics of a teaching culture), through the development of certain abilities, e.g. to create certain psychomotor activities and spaces (characteristic of a training culture), or by supporting the change of educational practice while simultaneously developing certain competencies. These competencies might include: observing and documenting the ways in which young children move; supporting children's development without stimulating and regulating their movements; creating a dialogue with families and other partners; and so on. In our case study, we decided to create and establish an approach centred on educational practice and conditions, hoping to develop a set of new competencies related to freedom of movement, an approach to young children seldom practised by families and professionals.

Several characteristics of this approach can be highlighted. First, it is important to note who the organizers of this approach are: not recognized trainers from an official training institute with a subject specialism (in this case, freedom of movement), but an ONE coordinator and an educational adviser without a specific training role, who had to combine certain traditional and somewhat contradictory functions (control, evaluation and 'accompaniment') with the development of this initiative. These ONE agents developed a partnership with another local coordination association, likewise without a specific training mission, and invited a specialist in the freedom of movement approach to provide some essential knowledge training to practitioners from both organizations. This partnership shows some characteristics of the culture of professionalization: the main actors are not themselves necessarily 'experts' or trainers, but workers who could improve and sustain the competencies of other workers (and themselves) by 'accompanying' the changes implemented in practice and theory. In this case, knowledge is regarded as an important resource, but not as the key to the resultant action.

Second, we can identify a change in the relationships between those involved: not only in the relationship between the teacher or trainer and each learner (a hierarchical or vertical relationship) but also between the practitioners themselves in a new network, where coordinators and an educational adviser are involved in the educational process. A horizontal, dynamic process is created and thereby transforms the traditional vertical control system. In this case, it was decided to propose certain actions to all the day-care centres in the coordinator's sector, rather than just to the observed voluntary practitioners. The aim was to give everybody the opportunity to exchange experience, and to actively debate different ways of acting and thinking. This initiative could potentially lead to positive changes, if certain conditions could be guaranteed. These conditions might include the requirement to: consider (some) existing knowledge (it is not sufficient to create and to invent alone); ground the exchange of points of view in documented practice and observation; analyze the effects of practice; evaluate and regulate practice; attempt to disprove or confirm hypotheses concerning different courses of action; and so on. This kind of process needs time and rigorous organization, both in teams and between teams.

Third, we must emphasise the action-research process and the principle of learning by doing. So the workspace, especially the day-care services, can be viewed as a professional space where practitioners who experiment with new practice and analyse their effects on children, families and themselves could not only improve the daily educational conditions, but also develop new competencies. In this case, during a first period spread over eight months, meetings were organized once a month both within each service and between services in the sector, coordinated by the ONE supervisor. The aim was to develop, implement and adjust action projects that would improve the movement and experimentation of children under 18 months of age. Every meeting between services was conducted by the educational adviser and the ONE coordinator, with the participation of a contact person known for her work on the subject. The five day-care services in the sector of the ONE coordinator participated in the process. As a first step they developed team action projects to promote opportunities for movement and experimentation by the children (the layout of space, the choice of games and objects to be manipulated, etc.). Once this was completed, they then made videos and analyzed the use of space and materials by the children, before finally assessing their own actions, both in teams and between teams. This self-regulating participatory assessment (Ballion et al. 1989), inspired by the work of 'Centre de Recherche de l'Education Spécialisée et de l'Adaptation Scolaire' (CRESAS, 1988, 2000; Hardy, Belmont, and Noël-Hureaux, 2011), allowed practitioners to adjust their actions and to understand the impact they were having, in a deeper way. In the culmination of the project, the teams shared – through videos – the results of their research with other professionals and with the families of service users at a local level.

The action-research process supposes an evolutionary view of the times and spaces in which we work, and of learning. New key players and new institutions can be identified during the process and involved both because of their interest in the theme (freedom of movement) and because of their power to facilitate positive change. New developments that could not be anticipated at the beginning of the project can thereby be conceptualized: new contributors, new actions and new networks that come together to adjust their shared approach.

From 2004 until the present day, this process has been extended to other childcare services and practitioners, including family day-care services. The work has been extended for several years, with other theoretical and practical approaches not mentioned in the curriculum: not only Pikler (2006), but also Coeman, Raulier, and de Frahan (2004) and Aucouturier's (2005) approaches. New tools and techniques to support analysis were trialled (e.g. photographs). From 2004 onwards, the sharing of experimental results with other professionals and teachers has generated an extensive debate, raising a number of pertinent questions. What kind of knowledge has been taught during initial training (for example regarding freedom of movement for young children)? How are students trained as future professionals? How can care service practitioners and school teachers 'accompany' students in a more collaborative way? In other words, how is theory meaningfully linked to practice? This project led to collaboration between the day-care services, initial training institutes and ONE with the objective of creating new and innovative ways to 'teach and train' students.

From 2004 onwards, the debate has also concerned physicians worried by the effects of a prolonged supine position on the development of young children (Cavalier and Picaud 2008). This led not only to the provision of information and debate sessions, but also directly influenced decisions to adjust the official information given to families in the French Community of Belgium (one of ONE's missions) accordingly.

It is clear that this process of innovation would need to be sustained over a period of time in order to be adapted to different contexts, and to strengthen the process without simply normalizing practice. This approach has itself raised a series of questions:

- How to 'accompany' professionals to regulate their educational practice based on shared criteria, as opposed to external standards imposed by the funding agency (Vial 2001)? This question is particularly important in a context where institutions and contributors had to link control, assessment and 'accompaniment' functions to achieve service quality.

- How to avoid reducing 'freedom of movement' to a homogeneous educational standard which professionals would be compelled to apply in all places and all circumstances, potentially leading to conflict with some families who hold competing values?
- How to involve families in the analysis of educational practice and its adjustment?

These questions base new approaches in contexts where the relationships with parents and families are currently poorly developed and where traditional approaches separate the private space of families and the public space of day-care services without considering real exchange. New approaches need to 'deal reflexively with complex situations and to construct practical knowledge in interaction with children, parents and colleagues' (Peeters and Vandenbroeck 2011, 70):

- Finally, how to build together action projects that not only improve the daily educational conditions of children, but also transform wider social relationships between adults, children, professionals and families?

Conclusion

The three educational action cultures, and the case study presented, are intended to be viewed not as a model, but rather as a support or tool in understanding some important changes in the field of education and training. They illustrate new trends in the French-speaking countries (and perhaps more widely), where 'accompaniment' is more and more often developed as a social and educational function in roles that were previously viewed as ancillary to training, and the development of the training market. Organizations that specialise in teaching and training use a wide variety of styles and methods to develop the knowledge, abilities, skills and competencies of day-care service practitioners throughout Europe. The report of the Education, Audiovisual and Culture Executive Agency (EACEA 2009) illustrated that official and political views and understandings of training activities vary between European countries. However, it is also important to recognize the value of less formal training methods included in the development of services and in the transformation of staff roles, which are not always labelled as 'training' or 'teaching' actions. For Barbier (2005), the culture of professionalization is not a substitute for the cultures of teaching and training; rather the three cultures coexist in a new configuration.

These new trends generate a number of questions. What is a learner or a practitioner in a process where everybody could learn together and from one another? Where are children and families placed in the process? How could we describe the relationships between the development of services (including quality aims) and the development of professionalization (including individual and collective competencies)? How do training actions undertaken within different learning cultures relate to one another? How could different kinds of cultures coexist in the same actions, and how could several educators work and learn together in a collaborative way? Amongst all these questions, the place given to families in the process appears to be a very important one, and should perhaps be recognized as a specific dimension in the construction of the profession and the development of services in the field of early childhood education.

Without compelling professionals to use specific ways of teaching, training or 'accompanying', the three cultures of education open new perspectives for understanding different ways to transform actors, actions and the learning/working environment. The challenge is to refrain from holding these cultures in contrast to one another: not to organize them into a hierarchy, but rather to use them to bring together traditionally separate frameworks, studying the individual and collective levels holistically, and integrating questions about the development of competencies and services into the process of education design.

References

Accueillir les tout-petits, oser la qualité [Welcoming the early years: taking up the challenge of quality]. 2002. Bruxelles: ONE-Fonds Houtman.

Aucouturier, B. 2005. *La méthode Aucouturier* [The Aucouturier method]. Bruxelles: De Boeck.

Ballion, M., O. Baudelot, B. Helmont, N. Bouvier, M. Hardy, F. Plato, S. Rayna, C. Royo, M. Stambak, and A. Vérillon. 1989. *Auto-évaluation régulatrice, une méthode d'évaluation pour les recherches-actions, Etapes de la recherche* [Regulatory self assessment, an evaluation methodology for action research, research steps]. Paris: INRP.

Baudelot, O., and S. Rayna. 2000. *Coordinateurs et coordination de la petite enfance dans les communes* [Coordinators and coordination of early childhood in the municipalities]. Paris: INRP.

Baudelot, O., S. Mayer, T. Musatti, and S. Rayna. 2002. A comparative analysis of the function of coordination of early childhood education and care in France and in Italy. *Early Years An International Journal of Research and Development* 5: 32–48.

Barbier, J.M. 2005. Voies nouvelles de professionnalisation [New ways of professionalization]. In *La professionnalisation en actes et en questions* [Professionalization in actions and questions], ed. M. Sorel and R. Wittorski, 121–34. Paris: L'Harmattan.

Barbier, J.M. 2009. Ingénierie et formation: Détermination d'objectifs, élaboration de projets, évaluation d'action, évaluation de transfert [Engineering and training: fixing goals, elaborating projects, action assessment and transfer assessment]. In *Encyclopédie de la formation*, ed. J.M. Barbier, E. Bourgeois, G. Chapelle, and J.C. Ruano-Borbalan, 455–79. Paris: Presses Universitaires de France.

Barbier, J.M. in press. *Vocabulaire d'analyse des activités* [Vocabulary of analysis of activities]. Paris: Presses Universitaires de France.

Beauvais, M. 2008. Accompagner, c'est juger [Accompany is to evaluate]. *Education Permanente* 175: 123–35.

Bennett, J. 2010. Nouvelles perspectives des études internationales sur la petite enfance [New perspectives in international studies on early childhood]. *Revue internationale d'éducation de Sèvres* 53: 31–41.

Bourgeois, E. 1996. Identité et apprentissage [Identity and learning]. *Education Permanente* 128: 27–35.

Brougère, G. 2010. *Parents, pratiques et savoirs au préscolaire* [Parents, practice and knowledge in early childhood education and care]. Bruxelles: Peter Lang.

Cameron, C., and P. Moss. 2007. *Care work in Europe: Current understandings and future directions*. London: Routledge.

Cavalier, A., and J.C. Picaud. 2008. Prévention de la céphalieposturale [positional plagiocephaly in primary care]. *Archives de Pédiatrie* 15: S20–4.

Children in Europe. 2008. *Young children and their services: Developing a European approach. A Children in Europe Policy paper.*

Coeman, A., H. Raulier, and M. de Frahan. 2004. *De la naissance à la marche. Les étapes du développement psychomoteur de l'enfant* [From birth to walking stages of psychomotor development of children]. Bruxelles: a.s.b.l. Etoile d'Herbe.

Centre de Recherche de l'Education Spécialisée et de l'Adaptation Scolaire (CRESAS). 1988. *Partenaires de connaissance. guide pour analyser en équipe les actions éducatives* [Partners of knowledge: A guide for analysing educational activities as a team]. Paris: INRP.

Centre de Recherche de l'Education Spécialisée et de l'Adaptation Scolaire (CRESAS). 2000. *On n'enseigne pas tout seul* [We do not teach alone]. Paris: INRP.

Dalhberg, G., and P. Moss. 2005. *Ethics and politics in early childhood education and care: Postmodern perspectives.* London: RoutledgeFalmer.

Dalli, C., and M. Urban. 2010. *Professionalism in early childhood education.* London: Routledge.

Education, Audiovisual and Culture Executive Agency (EACEA). 2009. *Early childhood education and care in Europe: Tackling social and cultural inequalities.* Brussels: Eurydice Network.

European Commission Childcare Network. 1996. *Quality targets in services for young children.* Brussels: European Commission.

Hardy, M., B. Belmont, and E. Noël-Hureauxeds. 2011. *Des recherches-actions pour changer l'école* [Action-research to change the school]. Paris: L'Harmattan.

Leseman, P. 2009. The impact of high quality care and the development of young children: Review of the literature. In *Early childhood education and care in Europe: Tackling social and cultural inequalities*, 17–50. Brussels: Education, Audiovisual and Culture Executive Agency.

Moss, P., G. Dalhberg, and A. Pence. 2002. Getting beyond the problem with quality. *European Early Childhood Education Research Journal* 8, no. 2: 103–15.

Musatti, T., and S. Mayer. 2003. *Ilcoordinamentodeiservizi educative per l'infanzia. Unefunzioneemergente in Italia e in Europa.* Bergamo, Italy: Edizioni Junior.

Oberhuemer, P. 2005. Conceptualising the early pedagogue: Policy approaches and issues of professionalism. *European Early Childhood Education Research Journal* 13, no. 1: 5–16.

Oberhuemer, P., I. Schreyer, and M.J. Neuman. 2010. *Professionals in early childhood education and care systems: European perspectives and profiles.* Farmington Hills, Leverkusen Opladen, MI: Barbara Budrich.

OECD. 2006. *Starting strong II: Early childhood education and care.* Paris: Organisation for Economic Cooperation and Development.

Paul, M. 2005. *L'accompagnement: Une posture professionnelle spécifique* [Accompaniment: A specific professional posture]. Paris: L'Harmattan.

Peeters, J. 2008. *The construction of a new profession: A European perspective on professionalism in early childhood education and care.* Amsterdam: SWP Publishers.

Peeters, J., and M. Vandenbroeck. 2011. Child care practitioners and the process of professionalization. In *Professional issues, leadership and management in the early years*, ed. L. Miller, 62–76. London: Sage Publications.

Penn, H. 2009. *Early childhood education and care: Key lessons from research for policy makers.* Brussels: NESSE.

Pikler, E. 2006. *Unfolding of infants' natural gross motor development: Resources for infant educators.* Los Angeles: Murray Circle.

Pirard, F. 2007. L'accompagnement professionnel face aux enjeux de qualité de services [Professional accompaniment towards quality challenge in the services]. In *Repenser l'éducation des jeunes enfants*, ed. G. Brougère and M. Vandenbroeck, 225–43. Brussels: Peter Lang.

Pirard, F. 2011a. Guide méthodologique Erato: Accueillir la diversité dans les milieux d'accueil de l'enfance (0–6 ans) [Analyse, evaluate and innovate. A guide for early childhood education and care (0–6)]. Analyser, évaluer, innover. Introduction, *Le Furet* (Suppl.): 5–8.

Pirard, F. 2011b. From the curriculum framework to its dissemination: The accompaniment of educational practices in care facilities for children under three years. *European Early Childhood Education Research Journal* 9, no. 2: 253–66.

Rayna, S., C. Bouve, and P. Moisset. 2009. *Pour un accueil de qualité de la petite enfance: quel curriculum?* [Toward a host of quality early childhood curriculum what?]. Toulouse: Eres.

Rinaldi, E. 2006. *In dialogue with Reggio Emilia: Listening, researching and learning.* London: RoutledgeFalmer.

Schön, D. 1983. *The reflective practitioner: How professionals think in action.* London: Temple Smith.

UNICEF. 2008. *The child care transition: A league table of early childhood education and care in economically advanced countries.* Innocenti Report 8. Florence: UNICEF Innocenti Research Centre.

Urban, M. 2008. Dealing with uncertainty: Challenges and possibilities for the early childhood profession. *European Early Childhood Education Research Journal* 16, no. 2: 135–52.

Urban, M., M. Vandenbroeck, J. Peeters, A. Lazzari, and K. Van Laere. 2011. *Core competence requirements in early childhood education and care.* Report for European Commission, DG Education and Culture. London: University of East London and Ghent: University of Ghent.

Vandenbroeck, M. 2009. Let us disagree. *European Early Childhood Education Research Journal* 17, no. 2: 165–70.

Vandenbroeck, M., F. Pirard, and J. Peeters. 2009. New developments in Belgian child care policy and practice. *European Early Childhood Education Research Journal* 17, no. 3: 408–16.

Vial, M. 2001. Evaluation and régulation [Assessment and regulation]. In *L'activité évaluative réinterrogée*, ed. G. Figari and M. Achouche, 68–78. Brussels: De Boeck.

Community-based learning to support South African early group care

Virginia Casper[a,b] and Faith Lamb-Parker[a]

[a]Bank Street College of Education, New York City, USA; [b]University of Johannesburg, Johannesburg, South Africa

The Developing Families Project-South Africa (DFP-SA) is a community-based model of education and training for the care, support and education of vulnerable children birth-to-three and their caregivers, guardians and families in rural and peri-urban townships. The approach fosters interactive learning among community members about early care and education integrated with HIV/AIDS education and prevention. This article focuses on the early group care component of the program. The DFP curriculum was co-constructed by the authors in conjunction with local parents and early childhood practitioners and trainers, based in part on findings from crèche observations and situational assessments of indigenous beliefs and attitudes concerning child development, early care and HIV/AIDS, implemented in five township settings across four provinces. This work is situated in the context of globalized educational practices with an eye toward meaningful integration of indigenous and Western ideas that together can help participants move toward consensus to improve care for this particularly vulnerable population.

Introduction

As women in developing countries are increasingly working outside the home, the numbers of group care settings for very young children are rapidly multiplying, creating an awareness of the need for education and training of the adults responsible for young children in group care (Park 2005). Women entrepreneurs are opening early care crèches, and adding on to already existing preschools to provide an income for themselves, while contributing to the growing need. In South Africa alone, the number of registered Early Childhood Education and Care (ECEC) sites has more than doubled in the past decade (Seleti 2009) and many other sites are not registered. At the same time, governments and organizations across the global South are developing initiatives, mandates and guidelines to foster the healthy and holistic care and education of young children, including those in group care (UNESCO 2010). Policy experts agree that the time has come for all corners of the South African Early Childhood Development (ECD) movement to mobilize creative and cross-sectorial programs for children in their earliest years and their families (Britto, Boller and Yoshikawa 2011; Marfo et al. 2008; Richter 2004).

Although infants and toddlers are a subgroup of young children, the attention paid to them has lagged behind even that paid to preschoolers (Engle et al. 2007). The World Organization for Early Childhood Education (OMEP 2009) acknowledges the lack of training for birth-to-three practitioners as a major barrier to improving early care and education in developing countries. Thus, despite the increasing interest and global knowledge regarding the importance of early well-being, the reality for this age group remains startlingly inadequate in many parts of the world, such as in South Africa (Palmi 2007; Richter 2004).

Given these conditions, the goals of the Developing Families Project-South Africa (DFP-SA) are to provide tools for *improving* the quality of group care for the under-threes; *integrating* HIV prevention and stigma reduction education; *strengthening* NGO capacity to educate, train and support crèche and preschool practitioners and parents; and *motivating* NGOs, preschools and communities to advocate for the unique strengths and needs of infants and toddlers and their families.

This paper describes the authors' philosophy and approach to adult education regarding birth-to-three education and group care. We highlight the complex and multiple contexts of ECEC in post-apartheid South Africa, describe our methodology and present initial results from situational assessments and pilot trainings. A discussion includes what would be required before such a program could go to scale.

Young children's lives in present-day South Africa

The context of the growth of care for the under-threes is nested within a country that is still a few years shy of 20 years as a functioning democracy. The legacy of apartheid still holds a tenacious grip on a country that has both developed and undeveloped aspects, with two separate and very unequal economies that still favor mostly white South Africans. There have been tremendous inroads made in the creation of a basic infrastructure of ECEC, but the catch-up is based on a governmental foundation that in its apartheid past had no ECEC policies of any kind, and a very fragmented system of services (Seleti 2009).

There are currently over five million children aged birth to four years living in South Africa, and over half of them are growing up in extreme poverty (Seleti 2009). Deprivation of adequate care and education are two of the top five risk factors on South Africa's Child-Focused Deprivation Index, and it is estimated that approximately 20–25% of black South African children under five are stunted due to malnutrition (Vorster 2011).

The poverty in most black communities in South Africa creates a complex series of interactions of vulnerabilities that causes very real and specific effects on children's nutritive, cognitive, physical and mental health as well as that of their families, including, most notably, maternal depression (Cooper et al. 1999). Vulnerable infants and toddlers may suffer from lethargy and withdrawal, requiring first nutritional interventions and then, where available, psychosocial supports for the infant–mother relationship (Berg 2000; Richter 2004). Young children growing up in poverty are at greater risk for developmental and physical disabilities, yet in South Africa helpful early intervention services such as speech/language or physical therapies are minimally available, especially in poor rural townships (Saloojee et al. 2007).

The overall child mortality rate in South Africa has lessened since 1997, yet the figures belie the still soaring death rates of young children, especially in the first year of life (McKerrow and Mulaudzi 2010). For the children who survive, HIV/AIDS is the leading cause of death. Malnutrition, poverty, lack of access to anti-retroviral treatment, if needed, and lack of adequate perinatal health care form their health context. Approximately 30% of pregnant women in SA are HIV positive (South African Departmentt of Health 2009), which rips apart family life and leaves approximately 1.9 million children under age 17 without their primary family of origin (UNAIDS 2010). Recent comparative data demonstrate that South African children and adolescents have rates of tuberculosis (closely correlated with HIV infection) that are at levels consistent with Europe a century ago, before there was chemotherapy treatment for tuberculosis (Wood et al. 2011). All of these risks, alone and combined, make growing up unscathed in South Africa a perilous obstacle course.

Conundrums of supportive work in early care and education

When collaborating with ECEC partners in a country outside one's own, the process of ongoing globalization and its effects on countries undergoing rapid change is starkly apparent. As Americans with expertise in education and psychology, working to improve South African early group care appears to be fraught with potential sinkholes as well as peaks of joint accomplishments. Over a decade of collaborative work with South African Non-Governmental Organizations (NGOs) across six of the nine provinces has taught us that all partners must be ever mindful of acknowledging uneven power relationships and need to work to reframe both conscious/unconscious racism and other historically based roles in a post-apartheid South Africa (Gray 2005). We often begin our work with new partners by asking, 'You might be wondering what we are doing here.' Invariably we hear that 'yes' that has crossed someone's mind. We share with them our love of their country, our work for social justice, in US civil rights struggles and supportively during the anti-apartheid movement, and what we have learned from our work in South Africa. From there, we begin the conversations, in which we co-construct a plan to study the local conditions and go about adapting a course of study with and about their community needs surrounding the under-threes and HIV/AIDS.[1] The training aims for participants to feel comfortable about challenging ideas that do not speak to their current practices or culture, resulting in lively debates. One training ground rule generated by participants was, 'agree to disagree and disagree to agree.' Examples of such dialogue concerning cultural vantage points will be included throughout this paper.

The tensions of globalization

There are many definitions of globalization and each one serves various needs. It does seem fair to say that the world is becoming smaller at a faster pace than ever before, creating 'accelerated compression' (Epstein in Gutek 2006, 99). Even what was once considered more purely 'local' has now been shaped, or at least touched, by some form of financial, geographic and/or power influences from afar. For example, specific concepts ('learning centers' etc.) used by many local ECD NGOs are derived from Western sources (e.g. High Scope, Montessori), but, more importantly, the larger theories and concepts behind them also commonly originate in the Western world (Penn 2011b). Thus, group care for the under-threes in many parts of South Africa is in itself a by-product of globalization, yet simultaneously based on thousands of years of socially distributed parenting and a rich history of maternal–child practices. We have noted, for example, that the traditions of large-group inter-actions, sibling/older children caring for younger ones and *ubutu*[2] now sit alongside caregivers' complaints about the personal, professional and ethical challenges of being responsible for such large groups of children under three, creating a classic 'both/and' frame of reference.

Globalization presents potentials for greater shared meanings and integrative growth while 'local' or indigenous experiences allow for a clearer sense of identity and purpose (Cleghorn and Prochner 2010). As elsewhere on the African contintent, centuries-old practices now sit beside newer options, creating multiple choices and often ambiguity where once certainty reigned (Barbarin and Richter 2001). Although we cannot possibly give the phenomenon of globalization its full due here, we raise it also to acknowledge that our collaborations begin with a joint assessment of local conditions, and that globalization processes are inextricably intertwined with what one considers 'quality' in a given ECEC program (Cleghorn and Prochner 2010; Dahlberg, Moss, and Pence 2009; Penn 2011a). We also agree with Super et al. that when 'developmentalists combine global knowledge of child development with specific understanding of the local developmental niche, creative interventions in the context of social change can be devised' (2011, 123). Through the DFP-SA integrated curriculum, global scientific findings (Shonkoff and Bales 2011; Siegel and Hartzell 2003; Teicher 2000) are combined with local values and beliefs, giving participants a deeper understanding and internalization of key con-cepts that increase the likelihood of sustainability.

Context of early group care in South Africa

In 2001, as part of an effort to address apartheid's legacy, the South African gov-ernment mandated that all five-year-olds attend Grade R (Reception Year) by 2012. Simultaneously, ECD NGOs made great strides in providing training to enhance the quality of black African township preschool programs for three- to five-year-olds. Nevertheless they remain located in the private sector. Fairly recently, however, the national government issued guidelines for the education and care of birth to four-year-olds, who until recently have been largely invisible in public discourse. While the programs vary in terms of the quality of services, resources and support, they are very valued by the communities in which they exist.

Beyond governmental efforts, a limited number of NGO organizations have begun to address the needs of this youngest population. For example, *Ntataise*, one of the five largest ECD training NGOs in South Africa, has conducted basic training courses in 'Babies and Toddlers' over the last several years for its 17 network NGOs located in seven of the nine South African provinces (Ntataise Annual Report 2008, 2009, 2010). Over the past decades, other NGOs have also offered training courses in infant care, such as those by ELRU, TREE and Grassroots Com-munity Trust. It is uncommon, however, to involve individuals in the community whose roles go beyond the preschools or crèches, and these trainings tend to have 'how to' approaches which often lack the 'why?' behind meaningful practices.

Discrepancies between crèches for the under-threes and preschools for three- to five-year-olds

Observations of preschools over the last several years reveal the stark difference between classrooms and programs for three- to five-year-olds and for children under three years of age (Casper and Lamb-Parker 2008). Classroom quality for older preschool children varies, but in most cases children are actively engaged in a number of richly expressive activities such as dramatic play, reading, singing and dancing, building with (found) objects, and outdoor water and sand play. Interactive communications with responsive caregivers and peers are common. Classroom walls offer a range of children's art, pictures of objects, animals, and schedules/transitions for the day's activities.

Rooms for the under-threes, however, are often small, and/or dark, with fewer materials for exploration. Under-threes are cared for in groups with large numbers of children and few caregivers. Ratios ranged from eight infants and toddlers with one caregiver to 50 toddlers and two-year-olds with one or two caregivers. These very programs tend to be part of otherwise well-functioning preschools for children aged three to five that reflect the years of training and support that South African NGO's have historically provided.

The caregiving practitioners

The women who care for the youngest children are eager for knowledge and skills in infant/toddler group care. However, they have few venues to discuss these issues with each other, few resources and they receive very low wages (Casper 2005; Casper and Lamb-Parker 2008; Engle et al. 2007). Despite the fact that many of these women are working in close quarters with practitioners who have been trained to work with three- to five-year-olds, most lack the basic knowledge or awareness that teachers in the next room may have. The shared plight of the practitioners and the youngest South African citizens is not lost on them. As one commented, 'the babies are on the bottom, and we are there with them' (Casper 2005).

Background of the project and history of the training communities

The DFP-SA was initiated in 2006, based on collaboration between the authors and *Ntataise*, a non-profit, longstanding exemplary early childhood development NGO functioning in mostly rural South Africa. *Ntataise* was founded in 1980 by Jane Evans to help women in resource-poor rural communities gain the knowledge and skills necessary to establish preschools for families with young children who were vulnerable to the effects of extreme poverty and lack of education. To date, *Ntataise* has trained over 20,000 women, reaching over half a million children, and, in the process, has strengthened the capacities of the rural townships it serves (*Ntataise* 2010).

The authors began the DFP-SA project based on previous staff development work in South Africa. Distinct lessons from experiences in both rural and peri-urban areas led to developing a new model with *Ntataise*. We saw how 'train the trainer' models lacked the continuity and breadth of community learning and the ways in which parent–practitioner tensions were a significant barrier to program quality (Lamb-Parker and Motsoeneng 2007). *Ntataise* chose four well-functioning sister *Ntataise* NGOs that could, in their estimation, take on the challenge of co-organizing and implementing situational assessments, classroom observations and a curriculum as well as co-conducting week-long training sessions.

The content for the qualitative protocols (i.e. situational assessments, focus groups, interviews, observations and curricula) developed out of dialogues and working meetings in the USA and South Africa. These included discussions with the leadership of *Ntataise* and the NGO staff, preschool parents and community leaders, and also with leaders in the early childhood, health and HIV/AIDS professional community in South Africa (DFP-SA documents and reports 2006–2011).

Methodology

Methodological approach

The methodological approach used by the DFP-SA includes three theoretical strands: community-based participatory research and practice (CBPR), community-based learning, and developmental interaction and transformative learning theories. The community-based participatory model of developing and implementing projects in resource-poor communities worldwide is an umbrella term referring to a range of approaches that include community participation, research and action (Lamb-Parker et al. 2000; McAllister et al. 2003; Minkler 2005). Research from the last two decades has made it very clear that the complexities of human problems require an integrated, non-hierarchical approach to change that engages populations of people where they are and builds consensus from there. CBPR was used to conduct situational assessments in respect of community attitudes, values, interests, observed and relayed behaviors and needs, on which the DFP curriculum was based. The model includes many important features that increase the potential for sustained practice after the initial project has ended. Among these are: (a) building local capacity to conduct research to identify needs in their community and to seek solutions, (b) creating ownership that ensures greater accountability during the implementation and after outside support is withdrawn, (c) fostering community strength and unity through championing common goals, and (d) empowering people to continue to make important decisions concerning all areas of their lives and those of their children and families (e.g. McAllister et al. 2003; Turnball, Friensen and Ramirez 1998).

Community-based learning evolved in part from seminal theoretical contributions by Urie Bronfenbrenner (1979), Paolo Freire (1970), and Kurt Lewin (1946) concerning the importance of community-based learning for both meaning and sustainability. Our model emphasizes experiential learning (role plays, small-group discussion, debate, and videos of local crèche practices). This approach enables the community to grapple with important issues, first within the safety of small-group discussions and then by sharing with a larger group.

A combined curriculum of HIV/AIDS and ECEC opens opportunities for candid discussions that would not be possible within a standard curriculum in lecture format. When this kind of integrated learning occurs among individuals with different societal roles, they tend to make connections with people they might not usually come to know, and have opportunities to do perspective taking on how others conceptualize such topics, and at times compassion for 'the other.' Thus, there is a greater potential to spread related ideas, facts and dispositions throughout the community. This is preferable and potentially more effective than having practitioners who are typically the recipients of such 'trainings' remain the only keepers of the knowledge. Having distributed knowledge means that knowledge is spiraled as it moves dynamically through the community regardless of one's role (Busse and Wesley 2006) or how long one remains in the ECEC community.

The DFP approach also is based on principles of developmental interaction (Nager and Shapiro 2000). Developmental interaction emphasizes that the dynamic relationship of children and adults in interaction with their environments serves as the centerpiece of any curriculum. Decades before we had the neuro-scientific data to back it up, this approach accentuated the ways in which emotion and cognition are inextricably intertwined in teaching and learning processes. This is not simply 'learning by doing' but, rather, encourages the learner to have experiences, reflect on those experiences and find meaning in them that can be put to use for action in the world. It is always the teacher, however, who creates learning opportunities and facilitates them (Dewey 1938/1997).

Mezirow's (1991) transformative adult learning theories also have particular relevance for populations of mature adults in South African communities who, based on a historically restrictive education system, have a lack of experience articulating their own thinking processes. In a similar vein, Davis-Manigaulte, Yorks and Kasl refer to 'expressive ways of knowing' that 'requires a healthy adult interdependence between affective and rational ways of knowing' (2006, 27). This approach melds well with ECD training, which is known for its vibrancy and active learning.

Knowledge utilization theory too has also helped us think about how learning becomes knowledge that is used in practice. Research in this area demonstrates that knowledge is more likely to be remembered and applied the closer the site of learning is to the site of its application (Winton 2006).

Participants

Five sites are involved in DFP-SA projects in four of South Africa's nine provinces: Thusanang Trust (Limpopo), Sithuthukile Educare (Mpumalanga), Tshepang Trust and MUCPP (Free State), and Kelru (Gauteng). Three are situated in rural townships, and two sites (MUCPP and Kelru) are in a peri-urban setting. Each is associated with between 10 and 40 preschools and crèches. Participating preschools were selected by the NGO based on criteria such as the level of functioning.

Between 2006 and 2011 the authors and program staff observed 88 early childhood settings (classrooms for three-fives; and rooms for the under-threes). Over 200 people participated in 54 focus groups and 76 individual interviews. The focus groups ranged in size from 14 to 20, and were made up of parents and community members connected with the preschools, health center, NGOs and community organizations in proximity to the NGO. The groups were made up of people of different ages, economic levels (but all relatively low income), educational backgrounds and experiences, and differing roles and responsibilities.

Although participants and participant groups were purposive samples and not randomly selected, they were formed with thoughtful criteria co-developed by the researchers and NGOs. These included: preschools that were well established for three- to five-year-olds; those serving a sizeable number of under-three-year-olds; practitioners; and parents of crèche-attending children under three. Stakeholders were selected among those who were known to the NGOs and who worked in health, education or social services in the immediate municipal and sub-district levels. Mangaung University Community Partnership Program (MUCPP) joined in 2009. This NGO is unaffiliated with *Ntataise* and is in itself a collaborative entity aligned with 25 crèches.

Procedures

Each NGO recruited participants for focus groups and interviews before the team's arrival and received their informed verbal consent. Administrative staff and trainers from the NGO participated in the individual interviews, which were conducted in English, with some clarification in their native languages (i.e. Zulu, Sotho). Interviews were also conducted with key stakeholders in the community. Focus groups took place in a combination of English and native languages, while parent focus groups were conducted solely in their native languages, with translation. Named 'listening and sharing groups' by the local communities, these focus groups became the vehicle for community participation as well as for information gathering for the 'situational assessment.' Participants signed written informed consents, translated into a language that they could read. Occasional payment of local transportation costs was the only remuneration that participants received. Language spoken was tailored to the group, with most of the training sessions held in Sotho, Zulu and English, the indigenous languages of the majority of participants.

Methods of data analysis

Various analytic techniques were used for the formative and outcome evaluations. Quantitative data were analyzed using SPSS (i.e. simple statistics, such as means, modes and percentages). Qualitative data were analyzed using a combination of hand coding and the qualitative data analysis software In Vivo Themes, and subthemes were derived.

Process and outcome evaluation results

Working teams

The first step of the DFP-SA model is to set up a working group at each site and to give themselves a name, such as *Sesivukile*, which translates from Sotho as 'We are NOW Awake!' The community determines the best 'port of entry' for their particular needs. Four of the sites identified the crèches as the best vehicle to reach the most people regarding early development, group care and HIV/AIDS. The MUCPP working group designated the community health center in addition to preschools as their entry points. Additionally, Mangaung Township and international youth, as well as undergraduate Free State University students, were trained in basic research techniques, and together collected the data in Mangaung Township. In both projects (2008–2012), we collected and shared community responses concerning who babies are, what people believe babies need, as well as beliefs about pregnancy, health and HIV/AIDS, as the basis for co-developing a training curriculum (Lamb-Parker, Casper and Abbas 2009). The HIV/AIDS-related data will be reported in a manuscript in preparation.

'Being at the table' together became particularly salient for parents and preschool practitioners who often have only limited interaction. These experiences help break down the parent–practitioner tensions that plague the majority of centers, because some basic agreement evolves as to what is considered important for the care of very young children.

Situational assessments

Data from the first four pilots reveal that the early childhood trainers themselves had wide-ranging educational and early childhood backgrounds. Of a total of 20 trainers, six had not taken a class in childcare and/or development at either the high school or college level. Fourteen trainers reported that they had taken one or more college or high school classes. Seventeen trainers reported having regularly cared for individual children other than their own. Two reported that they had never taken care of any children but their own. One master trainer had completed several college-level courses in ECEC. Through the situational assessments, opportunities continually arise for airing differences of opinion and weighing facts against myth.

Values and ethnotheories surrounding the under-threes in group care

Among the participants in the first four workshops, there was a general consensus that all young children in group care miss their mothers, although most practitioners believe that may be only in the beginning. What varied in the data was how the practitioners respond to the behaviors that they see. For the most part, the ratio of caregivers to children is so high that caregivers say that they often end up ignoring crying behaviors. Some think that crying is a sign of being spoiled, but most understand those young children's reactions are related to separation issues. They say that they just do not have the time to attend to individual children's immediate needs.

Two practitioners' remarks are telling. One said:

> … you want to be teaching others, others want to be holding your hand and be comforted. But there is no time for that, and they cry. When they come to the center, they must sit down and play with the other children.

Another put it in the form of a well-known Sotho adage:

> I am not your grandmother's lap. This means I do not have the time or ability to provide for you what your grandmother might.

Respondents commented on three major reasons for the growth in care for the under-threes. Babies need early care that is safe, affordable and prepares young children for later schooling. The trainers' point of view is best reflected in this trainer's comment: 'parents feel that they want to expose their children to the community at an earlier age, so the child will already be familiar with [school routines].'

Specifically, it was thought that group care benefits for the under-threes include: regular nappy changes, potty training, identifying special needs, verbal interactions, building trust in others beyond immediate family, developing large-muscle skills, increasing curiosity about the world, facilitating development through imitation, developing spiritually, growing more independent, learning right from wrong, and overcoming shyness. The negatives of early group care were identified as transmission of illness, safety issues, and that children with special needs require additional attention, which is difficult to provide.

Benefits to the practitioners of group care include: parents of babies are appreciative and give gifts, enjoy singing to and playing with them, and 'we learn from them.' According to practitioners, negative factors in caring for the under-threes include: parents do not pay regularly, increased stress from caring for too many, and the need for more training and knowledge about early development. As one woman remarked, 'many women take care of babies and young children, but only a few have the "passion" … at crèches, they don't get love. There is no time for cuddling, no time for playing individually.'

Successful training strategies

After the strategy of training beyond practitioners, the utilization of local crèche videos was our second most powerful outcome. Trainers were responsible for collecting two 20-minute videos of each crèche before the training began. Everyday practice that was relatively 'closed' to others became more visible. In each of the five settings, the group promised to make constructive criticism, and not to laugh at what by some might be considered poor practice. Practitioners complained that they are not able to spend time with peers from other crèches, and the videos and ensuing discussions seem to go far toward meeting that goal. Some practitioners used the videos to better conceptualize practices they had heard about but may have not fully grasped. Such was the case in a video in which a practitioner sat and shredded newspaper in front of small children while they watched and fluffed up the results. Her colleagues helped her realize that although she had heard that this was a cheap and effective activity, ripping the paper *with* the children would offer a range of possible interactions that did not happen when she ripped the paper *for* them. Parents sat very still as they watched some of their own toddlers interact with others. Likewise, the module 'What can you do with what you have?' allowed participants to see examples of what others have done with indigenous materials and everyday objects. The impact of this exercise could be observed in the excited faces of the women and men as they shared ways to improve their own particular crèche practice.

The video clips were paired as exemplars of particular concepts, such as child–child and adult–child emotional attachments, self-regulation or room design. In one video activity, participants identified examples of self-regulation. They noted a toddler sitting removed from others inside a cubby after her mother dropped her off late in the morning when the room was already abuzz with activity. We are convinced that a video that described principles of self-regulation in a Western context would not have been as successful as videos reflecting local South African crèche culture.

A third successful strategy was to address the overcrowding in the groups (already articulated through the situational assessments) and very high adult–child ratios. Rather than having us as trainers/researchers raising what we believed to be a serious issue, we asked questions and let the content emerge through discussion. Towards the end of each training, as participants became more knowledgeable and felt closer, they began to strategize about how they as a community might begin to tackle the large numbers of under-threes in crèches, which they felt was a barrier to better quality care.

As content opens up possibilities for trust between parent, practitioner and trainer, sharing in learning activities allows participants to see parallels in their lives. Trust builds as participants first work in small groups to identify their life challenges and blessings through the metaphoric use of potatoes in a sack, an activity developed by a South African trainer. This in turn allows for the introduction of a fact-based HIV/AIDS 'quiz' game. Later in the week, the further development of relationships allows for talking to one's children about 'difficult' topics before moving on to the stigma of HIV/AIDS in their own lives. In the 'difficult topics' exercise, for example (see Table 1) women in small groups recall their own coming into womanhood, and being shocked and confused by their first menses, because no one foreshadowed this inevitable event, nor did many matriarchs dwell on it beyond a minimal salute to becoming a woman. In retrospect, women wondered how they might pave the way for their own children and grandchildren to enter into the adult world with greater understanding. Even more poignantly, participants described how their own young children and grandchildren seemed to know already a lot about condoms and their purpose. Talking about it loosened a thread that one could feel being pulled across the room, as they struggled to reconcile past traditions of silence with new cultural imperatives of candor. The connections to stigma and fear of discussing HIV/AIDS became explicit through further discussion. Table 1 lists a few activities that provide examples of other kinds of integrated learning.

We have observed that local South African women without much technical or emotional support for their daily efforts in caring for large numbers of very young children relish the exposure to big ideas and that these ideas help them better conceptualize aspects of their work. Participants also become less defensive towards those in other roles (e.g. they eat and talk together instead of remaining in their initial separate groups) and enjoy discussing how some aspects of their culture(s) are robust whereas others are changing. During the module about 'talking to children about difficult topics' one practitioner (also a grandmother) asked, 'why is it that we are very eager to whisper in the baby's ear when his mother has died to say "your mother has left us, little one, but we love you and we will take care of you." In what ways is this different from talking to a five-year-old about HIV/AIDS? Why are some conversations fine with us and others not so much?'

Other issues came to the fore with excited discussions, such as the role of encouraging multiple attachments in a life in which the ongoing presence of caregivers (parents and others) can be less certain. Not only is the 'self' embedded in one's larger community, but to some extent adults must be ready to take on caregiving of children who suddenly are without their adults – in the short or the long term. The ramifications of this point of view for attachment strategies in a crèche are complex and expanded our thinking.

Findings based on observations of crèches

In the first few years of our work, our observations were informal and lasted about an hour each. In the fifth and most recent setting, observations were standardized with a working draft of an environmental rating scale of our own creation that incorporates South African early care practices and appreciates innovations and creative uses of self and local materials. Observations reveal that, overall, the under-threes are being cared for in rooms with few materials. In general, there is little adult–child engagement by Western standards, yet there are intense peer-to-peer interactions. The most playful learning tends to arise from interactions between the children themselves (sometimes positive, sometimes not). The most crowded rooms with the greatest numbers of children tended to be more chaotic with less positive behaviors (more hitting and biting, etc.). These crèche rooms tend to be part of well-functioning preschools for children aged three to five.

An older caregiver sat feeding a baby on her lap while two junior toddlers hung on and climbed over and on top of her. Across the room two other junior toddlers began to fuss. The caregiver put the bottle down momentarily and raised both her arms, waving at them with excitement while singing. The two toddlers imitated her

Table 1. Sample of exercises from the DFP-SA integrated education and training session.

Content	Learning activity	Practical applications
Understanding Object Constancy when Working with 'Under-threes' Children under three years are generally not able to independently retrieve combined mental images and emotional senses of a loved ones the way adults can (object constancy)	'Love Memory' Exercise provides an opportunity to feel the difference between a sensory memory of a loved person and an integrated memory that includes a mental representation along with emotions/sensory memories	This forms a base for a deeper understanding of what attachment means experientially for the under-threes. Strategies such as asking a mother to leave her scarf or a bag when she leaves the baby in the crèche become less abstract because they are tied to actual experiences. Parents too have an easier time conceptualizing what sensory 'love memories' are like for very young children and how long it takes to develop the internal ability adults take for granted
Early Brain–Environment Interactions Early brain development and how early experience significantly affects the way young brains develops	'Neuron Dance' Because singing and dancing is such an everyday activity, this dance uses one's hands to represent the neural cell, the fingers becoming the dendrites, and the arm the axons. In a circle, everyone sings and dances in an exciting way, connecting and waving their dendrites next to another's. Then, they move slowly without singing and with fewer connections	The difference between a lively interactive environment and one lacking in interaction is palpable to the human spirit. Because almost everyone is a parent, this experience really hits home. Through post-activity debriefing it is apparent that participants both feel proud to understand a basic developmental neuroscience concept and are eager to discuss the possible ramifications for their preschools
Abilities that Undergird Early Milestones of Motor Development	'Components of Motor Development' Participants lie down (both prone and supine to see the difference) and then slowly get up. They observe each other do so and note what they need in order to accomplish the task (e.g. first rotate, then push, etc.). They 'feel' concepts such as developing tone, balance and muscle strength, along with motivation to move	Because there are few physical and occupational therapists to serve children attending rural crèches, parents, practitioners and trainers benefit from being able to not just name milestones, but to know where to begin to intervene simply when a young child is clearly delayed motorically

(*Continued*)

Table 1. (*Continued*).

Content	Learning activity	Practical applications
How Direct and Honest Talk About Difficult Topics Helps Children Make Sense of their World (Silin 1995)	'Talking to Children about 'Difficult' Topics' Participants discuss their own coming of age. What unfolds is how confused they were about basic body functions and the development of sexuality due to lack of explication	This is an example of a learning intervention that goes beyond the preschool, yet uses the preschool as a port of entry. Participants each share a conversation with a child that they plan to have a conversation with in the near future

and they began to giggle as the caregiver went back to feeding the baby while the toddlers continued to wave fingers and sing. Such skilled distal practice allowed this woman to communicate with five babies and toddlers at a given moment. As she was alone with many more children, she was not capable (no one could be) of responding to the other children who also needed her attention.

The most intensive observations (long half-days at each of 22 creches in Mangaung) revealed variation across programs, as was found with another Free State crèche/preschool study (Declercq et al. 2011). However, we could not find such variation using traditional environmental rating scales. The essence of our observations is given in Table 2.

Innovative practices

Some crèches demonstrated extraordinarily creative uses of the few resources to which they had access. For example, rice sacks were used as pretend play 'blankets' to cover 'sleeping' babies; a hanging mobile created from a plastic bottle with candy wrappers moved in the breeze; cereal boxes wrapped in paper were used as children's individual art portfolios; buckets or plastic tables were used as drums; pamphlets were used as drawing paper; and an old covered bedspring covered with blankets became a very popular trampoline.

Discussion: implications for education and training of the birth-to-three workforce

Without a full evaluation, we are left with a hypothesis that while this ECEC adult training approach appears to offer compelling learning, there are missing pieces that serve as barriers to follow-through. When trainers make follow-up visits with practitioners, follow-through seems more likely. Nevertheless, four out of five pilot communities have continued the training as parents and practitioners bring workshops based on the training to their local networks (churches, women's groups, etc.). In resource-poor communities this suggests an excitement about the meaning that the learning has for the participants. Futher roll-out of the DFP-SA project should allow for an expanded evaluative component of the crèches (pre- and post-training) using an instrument that is sensitive to South African crèche conditions.

Tremendous changes in early childhood are sweeping the global South. Historically, the practice of families caring for their youngest at home, a traditional custom

Table 2.   Sampling of key findings from Mangaung creche observations 2011.

Area of observation			
Indoor Spaces	Half lacked suitable sized indoor space according to South African guidelines	Half had at least 2–3 pictures of some kind on the wall (e.g. numbers, letters, Disney characters) – one quarter had more than that. Some had nothing, or a sole vaccination poster	
Outdoor Spaces	Almost half had some outdoor space used for children's play		
Human Interaction	Half usually responded meaningfully to children's cues	18% responded proactively and consistently to children's emotional cues	32% of practitioners rarely responded to such cues
Materials	Over 80% had no building materials, but 20% had some kind of three-dimensional materials (coffee cans/wooden slats, etc.)	Tremendous variation in quantity of soft toys from many to none at all	
Program variety included: routine care, indoor/outdoor, singing/story time and active/quiet needs of, etc.	Approximately 1/3 addressed a wide variety of program needs	41% incorporated 'some' of these needs, i.e. routine care and two of the learning/play needs	1/3 had programs too rigid or flexible/chaotic e.g. children might participate in the same activity all day

that is considered favorable for children aged birth-to-three (UNICEF 2005), is being pushed aside. As Tobin and his co-authors remind us in *Preschool in three cultures revisited: China, Japan and the United States*, 'preschools are a relatively new social institution charged with the task of turning young children into culturally appropriate members of their society' (2009, 1). They argue that in a globalized world some practices have become more similar across cultures, others more diverse and then too, new practices have emerged. In this work we must also consider the mobilization of a workforce around ideas of early group care that may ring true but where the related applied behaviors in a classroom will take time to develop.

Conclusion

Although 'nuts and bolts' training for babies and toddlers has begun (i.e. basic care, feeding, HIV precautions), and a number of extremely creative uses of self and materials are reported here, we know that group care for very young children is challenging work anywhere. In South Africa ECEC, our impression is that care for the under-threes appears to be an early work in progress. Some practices are based on experiences of working with three- to five-year-olds who have different developmental needs, which can lead to a 'push-down' effect, and in a significant number of under-three settings there appears to be a lack of understanding of the real developmental needs of infants and toddlers. As one caregiver remarked ironically, they are simply 'waiting to be three' (Casper and Lamb-Parker 2008).

Part of that caregiving preschool culture includes up to 50 very young children in a single room, often with one practitioner/teacher. It is a cultural expectation that in preschools children must interact and learn from each other as much if not more than from adult interactions. But infants and toddlers cannot care for themselves and each other in the same way as four- and five-year-olds, and thus crèches face an economic and ethical conundrum. Women who are mostly living in poverty can make a better living by enrolling more under-threes. It is hoped that advocacy efforts will allow the country to engage in significant public discourse about how to address both the economic needs of the entrepreneurial caregivers and the emotional needs of very young children whose mothers need them to be in group care to fulfill their own personal and economic development.

Acknowledgements

This project has received funding from Rockefeller Brothers and MAC/AIDS Foundations. Tremendous thanks go to the authors' South African partners and US colleagues Monica Hayes, Emily Soong and Laura Zellerbach.

Notes

1. The term 'community' has multiple constructions. Here, we refer to individual citizens in a given geographical location who have banded together with interests in bettering their local under-threes group care conditions. Usually crèches vote for their parent and practitioner representatives, and local NGOs recommend other interested persons who are not connected to crèches.
2. *Ubutu* represents a deeply respected African belief that 'I am a person because you are a person' – reflecting a historically more interdependent society than in the West.

References

Barbarin, O., and L. Richter. 2001. *Mandela's children: growing up in post-apartheid South Africa*. New York: Routledge.

Berg, A. 2000. Beyond the dyad: parent–infant psychotherapy in a multi-cultural society: reflections from a South African perspective. Paper presented at the Seventh Congress of the World Association for Infant Mental Health, Montreal, Canada, July.

Britto, P., K. Boller, and H. Yoshikawa. 2011. Quality of early childhood development programs in global contexts: rationale for investment, conceptual framework and implications for equity. *SRCD Social Policy Report* 25, no. 2: 1–31.

Bronfenbrenner, U. 1979. *The ecology of human development*. Cambridge, MA: Harvard University Press.

Busse, V., and P. Wesley, eds. 2006. *Evidence-based practice in the early childhood field*. Washington, DC: Zero to Three Press.

Casper, V. 2005. Beyond feeders and growers: changing conceptions of care in the Western Cape. *Journal of Child and Adolescent Mental Health* 16, no. 1: 55–9.

Casper, V., and F. Lamb-Parker. 2008. 'Waiting to be three': a model of training, care, support, and advocacy for infants, toddlers, and twos in rural South Africa. *Association for Childhood Education International's Focus on Infants and Toddlers* 21, no. 1: 1–7.

Cleghorn, A., and L. Prochner. 2010. *Shades of globalization in three early childhood settings: views from India, South Africa, and Canada*. Rotterdam: Sense Publishers.

Cooper, P., M. Tomlinson, L. Swartz, M. Woolgar, L. Murray, and C. Molteno. 1999. Post-partum depression and the mother–infant relationship in a South African peri-urban settlement. *British Journal of Psychiatry* 175: 554–8.

Dahlbreg, G., P. Moss, and A. Pence. 2009. *Beyond quality in early childhood education and care: languages of evaluation.* 2nd ed. London: Routledge.

Davis-Manigaulte, L. Yorks, and E. Kasl. 2006. Expressive ways of knowing and transformative learning. *New Directions for Adult and Continuing Education* 109, Spring: 27–35.

Declercq, B., H. Ebrahim, M. Koen, C. Martin, E. van Zyl, G. Daries, M. Olivier, R. Veter, M. Ramabenyane, and L. Sibeko. 2011. Levels of well-being and involvement of young children in centre-based provision in the Free State Province of South Africa. *South African Journal of Childhood Education* 1, no. 2: 64–80.

Dewey, J. 1938/1997. *Experience and education.* New York: Macmillan.

Developing Families Project-SA Documents and Reports (Authors). New York City: Bank Street College of Education.

Engle, P.L., M.M. Black, J.R. Behrman, M. Cabral de Mello, P.J. Gertler, L. Kapiriri, R. Martorell, and M.E. Young. 2007. Strategies to avoid the loss of developmental potential among over 200 million children in the developing world. *Lancet* 369: 229–42.

Freire, P. 1970. *Pedagogy of the oppressed.* New York: Seabury Press.

Grantham-McGregor, S.M., Y.B. Cheung, S. Cueto, P. Glewwe, L. Richter, and B. Strupp. 2007. Developmental potential in the first 5 years for children in developing countries. *Lancet* 369: 60–70.

Gray, M. 2005. Dilemmas of international social work: paradoxical processes in indigenization, universalism and imperialism. *International Journal of Social Welfare* 14: 231–8.

Gutek, G.L. 2006. *American education in a global society.* 2nd ed. Long Grove, IL: Waveland Press.

Lamb-Parker, F., D.B. Greenfield, J.W. Fantuzzo, C. Clark, and K.C. Coolahan. 2000. Shared decision making in early childhood research: a foundation for successful community–university partnerships. *NHSA Dialog* 3, no. 2: 234–57.

Lamb-Parker, F., and P. Motsoeneng. 2007. Preschools as nodes of support: case study of comunity engagement and empowerment in rural South Africa. Paper presented at the Zero-to-Three, National Training Insitute, Orlando, FL, December.

Lamb-Parker, F., V. Casper, and S. Abbas. 2009. Developing Families Project: building a model of training, care, support, and advocacy for very young children in South Africa. Paper presented at the the Sixth African Conference on Child Abuse and Neglect with Focus on Early Childhood Development and Education, Addis Abbaba, Ethiopia, May 4–6.

Lewin, K. 1946. Action research and minority problems. *Journal of Social Issues* 2: 34–46.

Marfo, K., L. Biersteker, J. Sagnia, and M. Kabiru. 2008. Early childhood development and the challenge of responding to the needs of the under-three population. In *Africa's future, Africa's challenge: early childhood care and development in Sub-Saharan Africa,* ed. M. Garcia, A.R. Pence, and J. Evans, 01–225. Washington, DC: World Bank, Directions in Development Series.

McAllister, C.L., B.L. Green, M.A. Terry, V. Herman, and L. Mulvey. 2003. Parents, practitioners, and researchers: community-based participatory research with early head start. *American Journal of Public Health* 93, no. 10: 1672–9.

McKerrow, N. and M. Mulaudzi. 2010. Child mortality in South Africa: using existing data. *Health Systems Trust,* 59–71. http://www.hst.org.za/sites/default/files/Chap5.pdf (accessed May 5, 2011).

Mezirow, J. 1991. *Transformative dimensions of adult learning.* San Francisco: Jossey-Bass.

Minkler, M. 2005. Community-based research partnerships: challenges and opportunities. *Journal of Urban Health. Bulletin of the New York Academy of Medicine* 82, no. 2S: 3–12.

Nager, N., and E.K. Shapiro. 2000. *Revisiting a progressive pedagogy: the developmental interaction approach.* Albany, NY: SUNY Press.

Ntataise Annual Report. 2008–2010. Viljoenskroon, South Africa: *Ntataise.*

OMEP and I. Pramling Samuelsson. 2009. OMEP newsletter in advance of World Congress, no. 47. http://www.omep.org.gu.se/news/Words_from_the_World_President/no47/ (accessed May 5, 2011).

Palmi, R. 2007. *The ReDress Consultancy South Africa*. ECD in South Africa. 2011. http://www.redressconsultancy.blogspot.com/2007/09/ecd-in-southafrica.htm (accessed May 5, 2011).

Park, H. 2005. Childcare policies and ECCE in developing countries. UNESCO: section for Early Childhood and Inclusive Education. http://www.sfi.dk/graphics/Leave%20network/powerpoint%20presentations/unesco.pdf (accessed June 25, 2011).

Penn, H. 2011a. *Quality in early childhood services: an international perspective*. Maidenhead: Open University Press.

Penn, H. 2011b. Travelling policies and global buzzwords: how international non-governmental organizations and charities spread the word about early childhood in the global South. *Childhood* 18, no. 1: 94–113.

Richter, L.M. 2004. Poverty, underdevelopment, and infant mental health. *Infant Mental Health Journal* 25, no. 5: 440–52.

Saloojee, G., M. Pholole, H. Salooje, and C. Ilsselmuiden. 2007. Unmet health, educational and welfare needs of disabled children in an impoverished South African peri-urban township. *Child Care Health Development* 33: 230–5.

Seleti, J. 2009. Early childhood development in South Africa: policy and practice. Presentation for the World Bank Technical Workshop of the Africa ECCD Initiative, October 26–28, Zanzibar.

Shonkoff, J.P., and S.N. Bales. 2011. Science does not speak for itself: translating child development research for the public and its policymakers. *Child Development* 82, no. 1: 17–32.

Siegel, D.J., and M. Hartzell. 2003. *Parenting from the inside out: how a deeper self-understanding can help you raise children who thrive*. New York: Penguin Putnam.

Silin, J. 1995. *Sex, death and the education of children*. New York: Teachers College Press.

South African Department of Health. 2009. http://www.avert.org/south-africa-hiv-aids-statistics.htm (accessed October 12 2011).

Super, C.M., S. Harkness, O. Barry, and M. Zeitlin. 2011. Think locally, act globally: contributions of African research to child development. *Child Development Perspectives* 5, no. 2: 119–25.

Teicher, M.H. 2000. Wounds that time won't heal: the neurobiology of child abuse. *Cerebrum* 2, no. 4: 50–67.

Tobin, J., Y. Hsueh, and M. Karasawa. 2009. *Preschool in three cultures revisited: China, Japan and the United States*. Chicago: University of Chicago Press.

Turnball, A.P., B.J. Friensen, and C. Ramirez. 1998. Participatory action research as a model for conducting family research. *Research and Practice for Persons with Disabilities* 23, no. 3: 178–88.

UNAIDS. 2010. Global report. http://www.unaids.org (accessed October 12, 2011).

UNESCO 2010 World Conference on Early Childhood Care and Education, September 27–29. Moscow, Russian Federation. http://www.unesco.org/new/en/world-conference-on-ecce/presentations/ (accessed May 11, 2011).

UNICEF. 2005. UNICEF medium-term strategy plan, 2006-2009: investing in children: the UNICEF contribution to poverty reduction and the Millennium Summit agenda. United Nations Children's Fund. http://www.unicef.org/about/execboard/files/mtsp_final_draft_-may_2005.pdf (accessed July 9, 2011).

Vorster, H. 2011. The nutritional status of South Africans. Health Systems Trust. http://www.hst.org.za/publications/nutritional-status-south-africans-review-literature1975-1996 (accessed October 12, 2011).

Winton, P. 2006. The evidence-based practice movement and its effect on knowledge utilization. In *Evidence-based practice in the early childhood field*, ed. V. Buysse and P. Wesley, 71–115. Washington, DC: Zero to Three Press.

Wood, R., S.D. Lawn, S. Johnstone-Robertson, and L.G. Bekker. 2011. Tuberculosis control has failed in South Africa – time to reappraise strategy. *South African Medical Journal* 101, no. 2: 111–4.

Socio-spatial practices in a Finnish daycare group for one- to three-year-olds

Niina Rutanen

School of Education/Early Childhood Education, University of Tampere, Tampere, Finland

This qualitative case study approaches early childhood education and care practices from a socio-spatial point of view. One Finnish daycare group for one-to three-year-olds participated in the study. The ethnographic observations from the practices are analyzed together with the ECE practitioners' audio-recorded team meetings and video-elicited interviews. The analysis focuses first on the practitioners' role in structuring the physical and symbolic space, then on how age is used as a category to construct divergences in spatio-temporal practices. The practitioners constrained children's use of the physical space and directed children's attention and interests with different emphases on 'activities with predefined objective and location', 'transitions' and 'activities with flexible objectives and locations'. Age was used to justify differentiated spatio-temporal practices. Practitioners supported children in their developmental tasks to enhance adaptation to the institutional order and routines.

Introduction

Space and place have been applied as theoretical tools to investigate childhood institutions and children's agency within the institutional constraints (e.g. Holloway and Valentine 2000; Olwig and Gulløv 2003). Ethnographic studies have shown how institutions regulate children's behavior with the spatio-temporal structuring of everyday actions (James and James 2008). Institutional rules are coded into the routines and classifications of space as well as the temporal use of space (Gallacher 2005). In addition to spatio-temporal structuring and routines as instruments of control, the recent ECEC literature describes more hidden means for exercising power. In practices, children are encouraged to take responsibility and self-regulate their behavior (Emilson and Johansson 2009). By applying Foucault's (1991) notions of power and control, studies have also focused on toddlers' resistance to the institutional order and have presented the youngest ones as active agents in cultural reproduction (Leavitt 1994; Gallacher 2005).

Here, drawing on critical geography and following Henri Lefebvre's work (2004; original work 1974), the main interest is in the 'production of space' in early childhood education (ibid., 37). According to Lefebvre (2004, 33) social space is a social product formed by the triad: representations of space (conceived space), socio-spatial practices (perceived space), and representational space (lived space). Following this *spatial trialectics*, here, a dynamic interplay is assumed between (1) *the culturally constructed meanings, ideals and expectations of '(good) childhood'* articulated in curricula and other documents on early childhood education and care (ECEC), (2) the *local level of practices*, and (3) *the children's construction of space* (lived-through experiences).

In this study, ECEC is approached taking the socio-spatial practices as the starting point for the investigation. Spatial practices 'embraces production and reproduction, and the particular locations and spatial sets characteristic of each social formation' (Lefebvre 2004, 33). In the spatial trialectics, this is the level of the empirically observable, the perceived space, the visible; it is the way space is appropriated and dominated. However, it is acknowledged that the physical space and observable socio-spatial practices are interlinked with trialectical interrelations and overlaps to 'conceived space' and 'lived space' (ibid.). In other words, ECEC practices are constructed on the basis of legislation, national and local policies, plans and curricula, all interlinked and mixed with the local culture, resources and the practitioners' aims and ideals. Socio-spatial practices are also constantly influenced and restructured by children's and practitioners' personal experiences and social relations ('lived space'). It is the users who appropriate and give meaning to space (ibid.). As the practitioners play an important role in this meaning construction and appropriation, here, the socio-spatial practices in a daycare group for one- to three-year-olds are investigated with *the focus on the practitioners' role* in structuring, defining, and implementing the spatial practices:

- How do ECE practitioners structure the physical and symbolic space?

The preliminary observations suggested that the practitioners use children's *age* and *age-related skills* as justification for differences in practices. Following this observation, the second question focused in more detail on the use of age in structuring the possibilities and spatial constraints for actions:

- How do the practitioners use age as a category for providing different activities?

The Finnish context for under-threes

The focus is on children under three, following the division in Finland between groups for under-threes and three- to five-year-olds, including different caregiver–child ratios: 1:4 and 1:7 (Laki lasten päivähoidosta [*Act on Children's Daycare*] 1973). In 1973 the division between *nurseries* and *kindergartens* was discarded, and both under-threes and three- to six-year-olds started to attend *daycare centers* or *municipal family daycare*.

Daycare has an institutional task that includes care, teaching and education aimed at promoting children's balanced growth, development and learning (National Curriculum Guidelines on Early Childhood Education and Care in Finland 2004[1]). Without mentioning age in years, the national and local-level curricula both present the 'child's best interests' as age-related, and at the same time, generalize and distinguish between the needs and abilities of 'younger' and the 'older' children (Rutanen 2011). In general, developmental psychology has provided a strong theoretical basis for the practices. It is present in the curricula and reflected in the production of the child-specific educational plans (Alasuutari and Karila 2010).

Ethnographic fieldwork and interpretative analysis of the practices

One group of one- to three-year-olds in one daycare center was selected for the study. The group included 13 children aged 18 months to 34 months and three practitioners: one preschool teacher and two nursery nurses. In addition, the group received short-term substitute staff and trainees. One child attended the center part-time. Seven of the children had started to attend within the previous month before the fieldwork began.

The fieldwork included observational field notes, video recordings, and maps of children's movements during a six-week period (130 hours). The video recordings covered both 'routine events' (such as lunchtime) and 'non-routine events' (such as play) (Brownlee, Berthelsen and Boulton-Lewis 2004). A selection of video episodes (mealtime, sleeping, outdoors, play and dressing) was presented to the practitioners in semi-structured interviews (Tobin and Hsueh 2007). Also, three practitioners' team meetings were tape-recorded. As the fieldwork was accomplished over a relatively short period, this study emphasizes the triangulation of data. The ethnographic observations are discussed in light of the interviews and the team meeting discussions (Atkinson et al. 2001; Rainio 2010).

The first part of the analysis focused on how the practitioners structured the physical and symbolic space. The observational field notes, interviews and recordings from team meetings were arranged, transcribed and entered into Maxqda qualitative analysis software. The analysis started with the observational data: all descriptions and notes about movements in space, routines and practices and discussions about time–space were coded in a preliminary coding. As it became obvious that most of the everyday actions were somehow related to time and space, a new approach was taken. From the ethnographic observations, it was possible to create three categories: 'activities with predefined objective and location'; 'transitions' and 'activities with flexible objectives and locations'. The analysis now focused on identifying and understanding the dynamics within these categories. The end result was a narrative of each of these, including a general overview, comparison with the other two categories and description and analysis of the events that provide both controversial and supportive examples for the characterization of the practices.

The observations showed that the practitioners reiterated, justified or reframed the boundaries of activities, routines and rules. What was common to these three categories was that in all of them *children's age* was used as a justification for socio-spatial divergences, and age-related expectations in relation to children's behavior were apparent. Following this, the second part of the analysis focused in more detail on how age was used as a category to construct divergences in practices. From the observational data, all events and discussions including some references to age were selected for more detailed investigation. After the observations, the interview and team meetings data were returned and all related sequences that would support, contradict or clarify the observations were discussed in relation to the ethnographic observations.

Written timetable in action

Indoors, the physical space included three rooms and a lavatory, a vestibule and a corridor with open lockers. The group shared an outdoor area with another group of under three-year-olds. Alongside the *shared spaces* among the children and the practitioners there was a restricted physical space for the practitioners (e.g. locked closet, office space). The lavatory, the vestibule and a bathroom for water play, shared with other groups, were restricted for specific uses only.

This institutional space was characterized as having various levels of plans as the guiding structure (see Lefebvre 2004, 'representations of space'). The fixed daily timetable and the changing weekly plan were posted on the wall. The weekly plan described the activities for each day at a general level: 'play', 'drawing' or 'water play'. The daily timetable assigned the activities to particular spatial locations at specific times of the day (Leavitt 1994; Gallacher 2005). It was materialized in the arrangements of the objects and furniture and recurred daily. The children also learned this routine. For example, removal of the beds from the closets was a sign of what would follow. The weekly plan and the daily timetable were vague enough to leave freedom for momentary negotiations. It is possible to identify different groups of activities where the practitioners structured the physical and symbolic space differently:

- '*activities with predefined objective and location*' (such as meal, nap, and some specific days: handicraft, playing with water in bathroom);
- '*transitions*' (such as 'circle time', dressing–undressing, arrival);
- '*activities with flexible objectives and locations*' (such as playtime, outdoors).

Activities with predefined objective and location

In the daycare center the physical space can be characterized by division into 'functional sites' (Foucault 1991, 143–4) that have specific designated uses (Gallacher 2005, 246; see Figure 1). Some activities were predefined for the entire group of children to participate simultaneously within a specific spatial location, 'a fixed functional site'. The very general objective was common to all; explicit examples were meals and nap time. In these activities, the furniture and other material objects *constrained the actions to a specific location*. At mealtimes, children had their own predefined seats and at nap time their 'own' beds. On some days, a particular activity or task, such as painting, was arranged for a smaller, selected group.

At mealtimes, different approaches were applied to achieve the general objective. In addition to nutrition, other educational goals were apparent, such as table manners. The practitioners discussed the arrangements in detail so that all the children would eat or at least taste the food. Practical solutions were discussed in relation to where to set the food, how to offer it, where to sit and how to talk to the children.

The practitioners *drew the children's attention* to the objectives with reminders. Silent surveillance was replaced by intervention if children did not proceed towards the objective in a certain time-period, or if they engaged in action that seemed to jeopardize it. The practitioners directed the children's attention with questions. In addition, surveillance was sometimes underlined verbally (see also Gallacher 2005, 254): '*I will come to sit and watch when you eat*'. Even when assistance was offered, the pedagogic aim was to guide children towards independent eating.

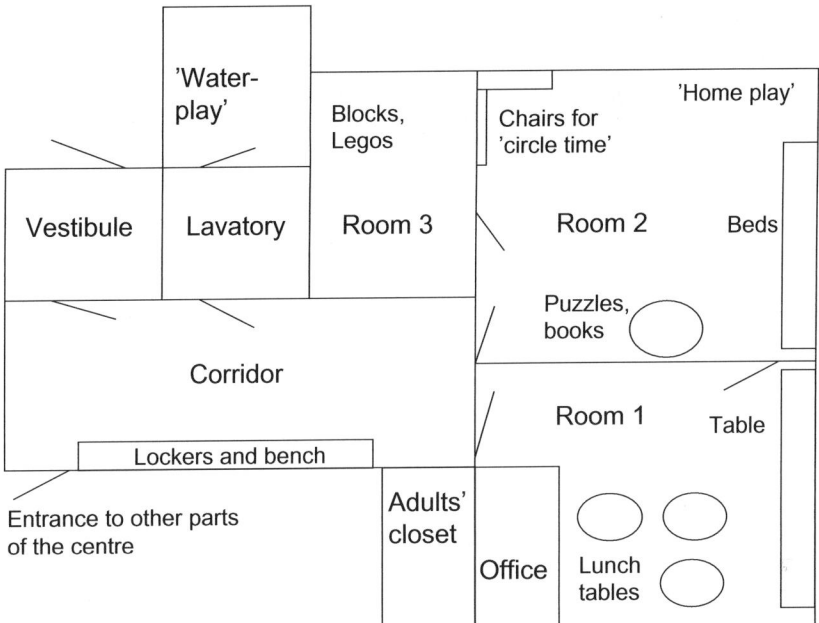

Figure 1.   Layout of the rooms. Note: Some details and locations of the rooms have been changed to ensure the anonymity of the center. The changes are not significant in the sense that they would influence the interpretation and evaluation of the data and results.

The mealtimes also included conversational initiatives other than food and eating. In addition to the children's initiatives, the practitioners introduced topics such as the weather or the forthcoming holiday. The function was sometimes twofold: both to engage in joint conversation and to divert the *attention away* from the topic that was presently elaborated. Typically in those cases, children were laughing or/and imitating each other loudly. The *sound space* was also structured with tools other than conversation. For example, at the beginning of nap time, a CD was played or the practitioner sang in a low voice. The practitioners used a low voice to indicate that children should be silent and remain in their beds.

The meals and naps were preceded and followed by '*transitions*' to be discussed next in more detail. At some point during the meal, for example, some children announced that they had finished. They tried to get up and remove their bibs. The practitioners attempted to prolong the meal if others were still eating or if the child had not eaten properly. In these negotiations, the child's seat turned into a *waiting place* for permission to leave the table.

In summary, the spatial practices described here include the practitioners' attempts to constrain, control and rearrange the spatial setting according to the pre-defined educational objectives. These processes of meaning construction and appropriation are deeply embedded in the social production of space (Lefebvre 2004), which goes beyond the description of the physical features of the setting (e.g. furniture, floor plan). Here, despite the momentary renegotiations and chaotic and 'free' moments following the flow of unpredictable events, the spatial practices were hierarchical, characterized by the objectives defined by the practitioners.

Transitions

The daily timetable allowed 15 minutes for activity that I would define as *'transition'*: 9.45–10.00 'Dressing to go out'. Yet various activities could be characterized as transitions between physical locations and activities. The children were usually invited *in small groups* from one location to another, such as to get dressed in the corridor for outdoor play. The practitioners justified the division of children by efficiency in controlling the situation, such as *'keeping it calm'*, *'avoiding accidents'*, but also by enabling children to practice their (dressing) skills without others *'running around'*.

During *'circle time'* the children gathered around one practitioner in a certain corner on small chairs to sing and recite rhymes before lunch. The practitioner also posed questions or continued the topic someone had initiated. Even the activity had a predefined objective and location, it was a 'transition' in the sense that the children gathered together to be sent later one by one to another room. Meanwhile, the other practitioner set the table and got the meal ready. Children had *temporarily fixed places*: once seated, the child was to remain seated. If the objective was not met even after a reminder, the practitioner took the child to her lap or moved the child closer to use physical proximity as a tool for control. A counting-out rhyme was applied to attract the children's attention, to keep them seated, and to underline the aim to learn to wait one's turn.

Dressing and undressing also occurred in groups of around three to five children. In the corridor the children had lockers marked with their names and photos. The practitioners often requested the children to 'go next to your locker' to wait sitting on the bench. Depending on the rush and availability of the adults, the practitioner paid particular attention to the child she was dressing/undressing: the discussion was directed at her/him even if the main objective was achieved in parallel. The topic was often the clothing, but also other topics such as the weekend. In these cases, the physical proximity afforded a dialogical space. As the other children were in a restricted physical space, a corridor with no open doors, there was less focus on overall surveillance. This observation is in line with Lefebvre's (2004) emphasis on the material embeddedness of everyday social space: the material constraints are not neutral in structuring the social relations that can develop in certain moments during the day.

On more hectic days the objective to dress/undress the children efficiently was emphasized. With muddy overalls and boots the practitioners developed a system of one receiving children in the vestibule, then sending them to the corridor for removal of the next layer and then further to the lavatory. In addition, while the practitioner was undressing someone, she gave advice to the others on how to proceed with the dressing/undressing.

The arrival at the daycare center occurred at different hours. On arrival, at least one of the practitioners focused her attention on the child and his/her initiatives, regardless of the ongoing overall activity. The situation was momentarily restructured according to the interpretation of child's needs: e.g. the child could sit on the practitioner's lap even if it was breakfast time, or receive his/her 'favorite toy'; even the rule 'not to take a toy from someone' was broken. When the children heard a knock on the door, they looked to see who had arrived or who was going to be picked up. The door represented both an entrance to forbidden areas but also a bridge between the private and the public space.

In summary, the practitioners directed the children's attention and interests with conversation, and structured the physical space by offering material objects (toys, clothes). Adding a new element to the situation served various functions:

- *to engage children in the activity at hand*. For example, introducing a topic for conversation during 'circle time'; handing over clothing for dressing;
- *to divert attention from something*. For example, posing questions and making compliments to the arriving child;
- *to engage children in something else for the sake of the main objective*. For example, offering books to keep other children entertained in the corridor while one was being dressed.

The corridor was restructured as a 'space for play' and the objects served as tools to focus the children's attention. The children were also given puzzles or drawing materials while they waited for the others to wake up from their naps. The practitioners remained close to children, ready to take the next ones to the lavatory.

Activities with flexible objectives and locations

For most of the day the use of the physical space was relatively open to momentary negotiations: the 'functional sites' (Foucault 1991; Gallacher 2005) were not fixed but open to children's initiatives and definitions. Following Lefebvre (2004), in the production of socio-spatial practices, different actors struggle for control over meaning. In the routines of the day care center, it was in the hands of the practitioners to interpret children's actions as initiatives and use them as a starting point for further restructurings of space.

The *outdoor area* was clearly delineated with fences, but within that area the children could mainly move without the practitioners' intervention. In contrast to the indoors, the outdoor rules were explicitly discussed and written down, since practitioners from other groups participated in outdoor supervision.

Indoors, the practitioners had designated some corners and areas of the rooms as *areas for play*, such as 'home play' ('playing houses'). Different locations had particular toys: books and puzzles on the shelves, a plastic play stove in one corner and so on. In practice, the children reshaped this spatial layout by carrying the objects to different locations.

During the observation period, the practitioners moved the 'home play' objects and furniture from the smallest room (room 3) to the main room (room 2). This was justified by noting how '*the home play doesn't fit* (there)' as '*these smaller children like to push things around*'. Building blocks were intended to enhance the activity at a certain location and the children would remain longer with the blocks in the small room.

When the children transferred the objects, the practitioners allowed them to remain in the new location for a while, suggested 'appropriate play' with the objects available, or suggested a more suitable location. To a child holding a plastic drill close to 'home play' objects, another room was suggested in a playful manner: '*Come here to this side and drill this chair, come and fix it, it's a bit broken*'. This restructuring occurred particularly when the children moved a lot, when there were many children in the same area, when there were signs of conflict, and/or the practitioners deduced that a child was not focused on some activity. If the situation seemed calm and the children were engrossed in an activity with objects, they were also able to use objects in new locations and for new purposes: e.g. a child's invention to put Lego characters on top of horse-shaped puzzle pieces was admired.

To divide the children into smaller groups the practitioners either invited some of them to a certain location or asked them to choose between different options, such as a puzzle or 'big cars' that also indicate a specific spatial location. One practitioner followed them, closed the door or sat close to the doorway to maintain eye contact in two rooms (see also Gallacher 2005, 245: 'hierarchical surveillance' and 'panopticism', following Foucault 1991). The practitioners negotiated over these movements throughout the day (see Karila and Kinos 2011).

The children often moved back and forth, particularly from the smallest room (room 3) if the others had remained in the main room (room 2). The children approached the practitioners, received comments on their objects and then returned to other areas. If the practitioner had introduced a 'play' (e.g. 'hairdressers') for some, others observed the situation.

In addition to constraining the physical space and dividing the children into 'play groups', the practitioners regulated *the number and type of objects*. If the children already had some objects related to a particular 'play', fewer new ones were offered. The practitioners removed toys if the play had moved to new 'theme' or spatial location. Children were encouraged to 'clear up the earlier play' before moving on to something else. However, the definition of *when* children had moved away from one activity/'play' was not clear. Often someone with empty hands was offered new objects, while someone who was observing others, holding something, was left undisturbed.

The practitioners intervened with verbal suggestions ranging from explicit prohibitions to playful engagement. To direct the action towards new or more appropriate interactions, the practitioners often applied a narrative of play, such as '*Look ... the baby gets upset when somebody yells!*' A similar intervention to offer new interests or location occurred if someone hurt him/herself and cried. The children were comforted, and often given priorities: they were offered object(s) that someone else also wanted or they could jump the queue for the swing.

The practitioners' *working hours* affected the restructuring of the physical space. Someone leaving often coincided with 'play time'. If the children were in different rooms, they were invited into the same room for surveillance. Similarly, if the practitioners interpreted that the situation was approaching a conflict or/and some other hazard was present, they used a preventive intervention, such as suggesting a spatially fixed activity (see the following extract):

Extract from the observations:

> Kaarina (the practitioner) was alone for a moment with the children. She sat on the doorway in between two rooms. Matias and Venla were pushing each other, it sounded as if one of them would soon start to cry. Kaarina asked: 'Venla, would you like to do a puzzle?' Venla followed Kaarina, and Kaarina gave the puzzle to Venla by the table.

Sometimes the children were offered an 'assistant role' to return the food trolley to the kitchen with the practitioner. They were allowed temporary access to an area that was usually out of bounds for them (Gallacher 2005, referring to Goffman 1968). This occurred if the practitioner interpreted that someone needed special attention, if someone was feeling left out, was missing parents or was ill.

Sometimes a small group of 'assistants' was invited to kitchen to 'calm down' the situation, provide some variation in routines, and/or facilitate the surveillance.

The 'playtime' and 'outdoors' were transformed into 'transitions' when the practitioners announced that it was time to collect the toys. Often they were already thinking of the next step and the use of objects was restricted accordingly. The practitioners usually announced 'clearing up time' quite well in advance of going out or going back inside. This served various purposes: (a) to prevent new activity with objects, (b) to orient children towards finishing the activities they were engaged in, (c) to teach the children to keep things in order, (d) to initiate a *shared activity of collecting*, and (e), especially outdoors, to keep the children entertained until they went indoors. Outdoors, the practitioners used singing and games as *waiting rituals*, with a similar function to keep the children close to themselves and entertained.

Age-related variations in the practices

The socio-spatial practices included making a distinction between 'the small' ('younger') and 'the big' ('older') children. At mealtimes and nap times the children had their own assigned places according to their *age and age-related skills*: seats either at the table for 'the big' or 'the small', and bunk beds either on the upper level for 'the big ones' or on lower level for 'the small ones'. The children nearing three years slept on the upper bunks. These *assigned places* were not permanently fixed. Sometimes 'the older ones' were told to give up their seat or bed and to go among the 'young ones' if they were not behaving according to expectations or rules. Access to the 'big ones'' table or upper bunk was presented as a reward for 'growth' or 'good' behavior. By reminding the child that she/he was 'big' children's behavior was guided in a certain direction, such as silence at nap time or eating unaided.

The 'circle time' was constructed as a closed space with the assumption of shared attention, singing together and rhythmic movements. To ensure this, the practitioners used preventive restructuring of the space: they often took one of the youngest newcomers on their laps. *The development of self-control and discipline, concentration and 'learning to wait for one's turn'* were particularly emphasized with the counting-out rhyme. Children were reminded that the attempt is to learn to go one by one. Often the 'small ones' were given priorities in terms of shorter waiting time. This occurred both in 'circle time' and in transitions from outdoors to indoors.

The practitioners used physical proximity as a tool for control and preventive intervention, but also as reward and expression of care. The 'youngest' children, who were often the newcomers in the group, were seen to require more *attention in order to learn the routines and skills*. In the following extract, the practitioner commented on some of the 'youngest ones' progress in these skills after observing the video:

Extract from an interview:

Ritva: 'here you can see this that after we have practiced this sitting (.) it is so nice to see that Lauri, for example, sits there quite well already (.) that he can remain for a moment (.) that he is one of the youngest and can follow part of the time (.) and then Matias, he (.) now manages to sit better and starts to focus a bit better.'

To explain why particular children sat on an adult's lap during 'circle time', the practitioner said: '*not because they must, but they in a way really like to be there*'. The narrative offered was able to interlink the capacities and skills to be learned and the developmental, individual needs of the 'young ones'. Physical proximity was 'good for the child' in all measures. Similarly, the 'arrival time' included an *assumption of emotional vulnerability* that decreased with age and adaptation. Children 'needed' fewer hugs when they were older.

The *lack of play skills* was discussed among the practitioners and they shared an image of a young child carrying things around a lot. Different objects were seen *as stimuli* and by restrictions children would learn to focus and concentrate on long-term play, without '*mixing things*'. The adults' model for the play was emphasized. However, at mealtimes the practitioners valued the 'big ones' as models. The possibility of the 'big ones' learning from the 'small ones' was not conceived of.

The skill of consideration for others was emphasized. Often the 'smaller ones' had privileges in relation to access to toys or locations and the 'big ones' were given explanations that emphasized the lack of understanding among the 'young ones'. The 'youngest ones' were also assumed to lack the social skills for creating a shared long-term activity. The practitioners sometimes intervened when they approached each other as the assumption was that it would end up in conflict, not shared activity.

Children's perceptions and knowledge of their own bodies was valued. Particularly in 'transitions' the practitioners enquired whether children needed to go to the lavatory, or if they were 'full' (of food). The assessment of whether these perceptions were accurate depended among other things on age and language skills. Following the age-related development and practitioners' guidance, children were expected to express their needs in more detail, especially in conflict situations.

The institutional setting proposed a certain ideal time-frame for the development of skills. The closer the child was to turning three years, the more emphasis was placed on the development of the skills that should be acquired before moving to the '*older and bigger group*', as is discussed in the following extract:

Extract from an interview:

Ritva: '. . . I was thinking that our Olivia, Venla, Arttu and Aleksi, who will be three next summer, that they will already be quite big and skillful in the spring (.) that, then, we can practice many issues that they will face in the big group (.) so that they would be more ready to face the big group that has many more children (.) there are many (.) that, maybe, it functions differently.'

And later on, during the same discussion, after the practitioners had commented about restricting children's running indoors:

Ritva: 'Well it is a bit like (.) I already teach them here a bit because they will be moving to the big ones' group (.) that you can't run a lot indoors (.) that this is something they have in back of their minds as a sort of knowledge.'

The older the child was, the more self-control, patience and acceptance of rules was assumed in addition to skills such as independent eating, toilet use and dressing. Since 'any space implies, contains and dissimulates social relationships' (Lefebvre 2004, 83) the spatial practices discussed here reflect *asymmetrical and hierarchical space and relations* embedded within divergent expectations in relation to children's agency within these spatial practices. Regardless of the visible boundaries (e.g. chairs and beds for 'young ones'), however, the space is not *divided* but there exists an ambiguous continuity (ibid. 87, 90). Space for both 'the youngest' and 'the oldest' children is negotiable, fluid and open to redefinitions.

Discussion

In Finland, the scientific production of knowledge about everyday life in toddler groups has been largely overshadowed by the interest in three- to five-year-olds or six-year-olds at preschool. The few studies that have focused on one- to three-year-olds during the last 15 years have been mainly observational studies with various thematic interests such as play, mathematics, music and sleep–wake rhythms (Hännikäinen 2010). A 'Kangaroo' project reported by Kalliala (2011) is an exception in applying a quantitative approach to analyze the role of the adult and the involvement of the child. The discourse of the 'competent child' is scrutinized critically, and an emphasis on adults' sensitivity is brought onto the research agenda (Kalliala 2011).

Internationally, young children's early sociability and agency have been widely addressed in the recent literature (Rayna and Laevers 2011; Trevarthen 2011). The material objects have been closely related to the analyses of children's interaction whereas the spatial aspects have received less attention. However, there are some exceptions such as the 'Day in the Life' project with toddlers from seven countries (e.g. Hancock and Gillen 2007). Some recent studies on toddler rooms and daycare centers have discussed how material and symbolic features of the setting and activities of the educators interact to orient children's experiences (Musatti and Mayer 2011, 208; see also Campos de Carvalho and Rossetti-Ferreira 1993; Legendre and Munchenbach 2011). Similarly to the results presented here, Musatti and Mayer (ibid., 215) observed that children sharing an attentional focus on an activity was 'a function of both the spatial arrangement of the setting and the educator's location'. The role of the environment, including the adult, was central in the attempt to accommodate, contain and possibly resist children's impulses to move around (ibid., 218).

By applying socio-spatial lenses to daycare, it is possible to gain some understanding of the network of powers realized in the production of this *institutional space* embedded with ideologies, practices and personal, lived experiences (Lefebvre 2004). First, the power of the adult in indicating the *forbidden and allowed* areas for children become clear: forbidden areas are separated by rules and boundaries such as closed doors and fences. Specific locations are accessible, yet restricted regarding *particular behavior and interactions* (no running inside). Furthermore, the interactions might be restricted to *a certain time* of the day (no walking about during nap time). Second, socio-spatial lenses serve to reveal the role of the *material* in channeling the activities. Furthermore, by detailed investigation of the time–space movements and routines, it is possible to interpret how the *discourses on childhood/toddlerhood* are realized at grassroots level. Finally, socio-spatial lenses also serve to point out that the daycare center is not a uniform, equal socio-spatial entity for all, but that each actor has a personal (lived) space within, around and aside from the shared through personal experiences and positions. These are complex processes intertwined in the production of social space that is porous and multilayered (Lefebvre 2004).

The article suggests that *socio-spatial practices* and *age as a social category* are interlinked with the guiding ideal 'the best interests of the child' (National Curriculum Guidelines on Early Childhood Education and Care in Finland 2004). Age is closely related to notions of *what should be provided* (security, assistance), to the expectations of *how fast the child is able to learn and adapt to the routines*, and *what can already be required*. At the beginning of daycare attendance, the age-related normative assumptions regarding behavior and skills are the starting point before personal relationships start to build up.

The practices include various tensions that emanate from the socio-spatial practices but also reflect the discourses linked to this institutional space ('representations of space' by Lefebvre 2004). First, the momentary negotiations included tensions in between the *governance of the group* and emphasis on *individual development and interests* (see also Markström and Halldén 2009). The second tension emanates from the requirement for *preventive surveillance and risk-management* that is deeply ingrained in this institutional setting (also Kernan and Devine 2010). At the same time as *protection* was emphasized, on the other hand, *promoting children's learning in new and challenging situations* was valued as a preparation for future adaptation to the group of over-threes where the adult–child ratio is different. As a result, the *ideal toddler* would learn to take care of him/herself independently (dressing, eating, toilet use, language skills), develop self-discipline, and follow the routines which reduce the need to actively constrain his/her actions as well as *his/her need* for individual attention from adults (see Gulløv 2003; Markström and Halldén 2009). In practice, some of the children were cases in-between causing concern or surprise: 'big' (close to three) but not speaking yet; 'small' (close to one) but well adapted since the first day; 'big' and talkative but having adult-like discussions only with the practitioners.

This study indicates that both initial and continuing professional development would benefit from reflexive and critical analysis of the socio-spatial practices and the *institutional structures* reflected in the practices. What are written and unwritten ideals and aims, and what are the realities in the practices in toddler care? What are the unwritten, dynamic and fluid re-structurings occurring during the daily practices? The study also underlines the importance of building critical awareness among practitioners into classifications and boundaries built in relation to children's age and age-related skills, as well as other categories such as gender and ethnic background. These categories and classifications are materialized in the actual socio-spatial practices constraining children's everyday actions.

Acknowledgements

This work was supported by the Academy of Finland, project *(In)visible Toddlerhood? Global and Local Constructions of Toddlers' Places in Institutions* 2010–2012 (project 133345). In addition to the anonymous reviewers, the author is also grateful to Kaisu Hermanfors, Kirsti Karila, Päivi Kupila, Raija Raittila and Mari Vuorisalo for helpful comments and to Kaisa-Reeta Laitila for her assistance in the data transcription.

Note

1. The National Curriculum Guidelines on Early Childhood Education and Care (2004) provide a national tool for planning at the local levels. Municipal-level and unit-specific curricula as well as child-specific plans are all being developed.

References

Alasuutari, M., and K. Karila. 2010. Framing the picture of the child. *Children & Society* 24: 100–11.

Atkinson, P., A. Coffey, S. Delamont, J. Lofland, and L. Lofland, eds. 2001. *Handbook of ethnography.* London: Sage Publications.

Brownlee, J., D. Berthelsen, and G. Boulton-Lewis. 2004. Working with toddlers in child care: Personal epistemologies and practice. *European Early Childhood Education Research Journal* 12, no. 1: 55–70.

Campos de Carvalho, M.I., and M.C. Rossetti-Ferreira. 1993. Importance of spatial arrangements for young children in day care centers. *Children's Environments* 10, no. 1: 19–30.

Emilson, A., and E. Johansson. 2009. The desirable toddler in preschool: Values communicated in teacher and child interactions. In *Participatory learning in the early years: Research and pedagogy.* Routledge research in education 21, ed. D. Berthelsen, J. Brownlee, and E. Johansson, 61–77. New York: Routledge.

Foucault, M. 1991. *Discipline and punish: The birth of the prison.* London: Penguin Books.

Gallacher, L. 2005. 'The terrible twos': Gaining control in the nursery? *Children's Geographies* 3, no. 2: 243–64.

Gulløv, E. 2003. Creating a natural place for children: An ethnographic study of Danish kindergartens. In *Children's Places: Cross-cultural perspectives,* ed. K. Olwig and E. Gulløv, 23–39. London: Routledge.

Hancock, R., and J. Gillen. 2007. Safe places in domestic spaces: Two-year-olds at play in their homes. *Children's Geographies* 5, no. 4: 337–51.

Hännikäinen, M. 2010. 1 to 3-year-old children in day care centres in Finland: An overview of eight doctoral dissertations. *International Journal of Early Childhood* 24, no. 2: 101–15.

Holloway, S. L., and G. Valentine, eds. 2000. *Children's geographies: Playing, living, learning.* London: Routledge.

James, A., and A. James, eds. 2008. *European childhoods: Cultures, politics and childhoods in Europe.* Basingstoke: Palgrave Macmillan.

Kalliala, M. 2011. Look at me! Does the adult truly see and respond to the child in Finnish day-care centres? *European Early Childhood Education Research Journal* 19, no. 2: 237–53.

Karila, K., and J. Kinos. 2011, forthcoming. Acting as a professional in a Finnish early childhood education context. In *Early childhood grows up: Towards a critical ecology of the profession.* International Perspectives on Early Childhood Education and Development 6, ed. L. Miller, C. Dalli, and M. Urban, 55–69. Dordrecht: Springer.

Kernan, M., and D. Devine. 2010. Being confined within? Constructions of the good childhood and outdoor play in early childhood education and care settings in Ireland. *Children & Society* 24, no. 5: 371–85.

Laki lasten päivähoidosta [*Act on Children's Daycare*] 36/1973. Helsinki: Ministry of Justice. http://www.finlex.fi/fi/laki/ajantasa/1973/19730036 (accessed 5 May 2011).

Leavitt, R.L. 1994. *Power and emotion in infant-toddler day care.* Albany: State University of New York Press.

Lefebvre, H. 2004. *The production of space.* Translated by Donald Nicholson-Smith, originally published in 1974. Malden, MA: Blackwell.

Legendre, A., and D. Munchenbach. 2011. Two-to-three-year-old children's interactions with peers in child-care centres: Effects of spatial distance to caregivers. *Infant behavior & Development* 34: 111–25.

Markström, A-M., and G. Halldén. 2009. Children's strategies for agency in preschool. *Children & Society* 23: 112–22.

Musatti, T., and S. Mayer. 2011. Sharing attention and activities among toddlers: The spatial dimension of the setting and the educator's role. *European Early Childhood Education Research Journal* 19, no. 2: 207–21.

National Curriculum Guidelines on Early Childhood Education and Care in Finland. 2004. Helsinki: Stakes. http://www.thl.fi/thl-client/pdfs/267671cb-0ec0-4039-b97b-7ac6ce6b9c10 (accessed 5 May 2011).

Olwig, K., and E. Gulløv, eds. 2003. *Children's places: Cross-cultural perspectives.* London: Routledge.

Rainio, A. 2010. *Lionhearts of the playworld: An ethnographic case study of the development of agency in play pedagogy.* Studies in Educational Sciences 233. University of Helsinki. http://urn.fi/URN:ISBN:978-952-10-5959-9 (accessed 5 May 2011).

Rayna, S., and F. Laevers. 2011. Editorial. Understanding children from 0 to 3 years of age and its implications for education. What's new on the babies' side? Origins and evolutions. *European Early Childhood Education Research Journal* 19, no. 2: 161–72.

Rutanen, N. 2011. Space for toddlers in the guidelines and curricula for early childhood education and care in Finland. *Childhood* 18, no. 4: 523–36.

Tobin, J., and Y. Hsueh. 2007. The poetics and pleasures of video ethnography of education. In *Video research in the learning sciences*, ed. R. Goldman, 77–92. New York: Lawrence Erlbaum.

Trevarthen, C. 2011. What young children give to their learning, making education work to sustain a community and its culture. *European Early Childhood Education Research Journal* 19, no. 2: 173–93.

What counts when working with mathematics in a toddler-group?

Camilla Björklund

Department of Education, Communication and Learning, Gothenburg University, Gothenburg, Sweden

An educator working in a toddler-group (children aged 1–3) took part in an in-service program using a 'Learning Study' design within the broader theoretical frame of the 'Variation Theory of learning'. The purpose of this study is, in qualitative terms and in the context of explorative play, to describe how the educator develops strategies where toddlers are given relevant opportunities to explore mathematical concepts. Results of the analyses highlight the effects of a heightened awareness of mathematics, as it is enhancing the opportunities to explore mathematical concepts and principles, but also how this can lead to an articulated awareness – demonstrated in interaction with the toddlers – that enables the educator to take the children's initiatives as starting points for planned education. It also highlights the need to use nuanced and adequate mathematical language in toddler day-care.

Introduction

Mathematics aims at describing relationships in space, time and number and works as a tool for communicating about such relationships. Studies of toddlers' self-chosen activities, play and interaction with others within day-care settings have shown how children have opportunities to encounter many aspects of mathematics (Björklund 2007; Björklund 2010a). These opportunities may be used by educators to support the development of children's skills and understanding of mathematics. However, educators working with the youngest children do not always show sufficient awareness of their role and the importance of their own approach to mathematics learning and the effect it has on the learning opportunities offered to children (Doverborg and Pramling Samuelsson 2004). Longitudinal studies show the importance for later achievement in mathematics of early caregivers' interaction and use of mathematical language and content in communication with children (Levine, Whealton Suriyakham, Rowe, Huttenlocher, and Gunderson 2010). Thus there seems to be a need for an improved awareness among educators of the basics of mathematics, the social and communicative aspects of mathematics, and how mathematics is experienced by children.

Björklund (2007) proposes, in her study of toddlers' self-initiated exploration of mathematical phenomena, the necessity of having a common focus in order for educational activities to be beneficial for toddlers. This means that the educator is aware of the child's perspective and what the toddler's attention is aimed at. However, the question that nevertheless remains is: How will it be possible to gain this simultaneity and commonness of focus?

In educational practice there is always an intention to explore and learn particular things. But when it comes to young children and learning, play and learning cannot and should not be separated in practice (Pramling Samuelsson and Asplund Carlsson 2008). This forms the object of inquiry for the educator in the current study where focus is directed to children's experiences and developing concepts of mathematics. The study is an attempt to analyse what is critical in creating spaces for learning, in which child and educator share a common focus, thus making support for learning possible.

Purpose and aims

The purpose of this study is, using a qualitative approach, to describe and analyse the educational work carried out in a toddler-group. The analysis focuses on how the educator develops strategies in her educational approach that involve toddlers being given relevant opportunities to explore mathematical concepts. The research questions addressed by the study are: What is critical in the interactive process of learning mathematical concepts in toddler day-care? What are the educational benefits of Learning Studies (see 'The project' below) in toddler day-care?

The first question will generate an analysis of collected videographic data material, in order to discern that which seems to be critical in the educator and child interaction and which constitutes education. These features are important to recognise in that they highlight aspects which must be considered when working with toddlers in educational settings.

The second research question involves a meta-analysis of the progress in professional reasoning that can be observed in videographic data, as well as in an interview with the educator.

Mathematics in the early years

The human child is born with an ability to discern changes in amount, shape, rhythm and number (Wynn 1998; McCrink and Wynn 2004). Although innate, these abilities of early mathematical reasoning will nevertheless develop in interaction with other people and the surrounding world. Because of differences not just in cognitive abilities but also in social background (Siegler and Ramani 2009), not all children develop their skills to the same extent. The relationship between early number competence and later arithmetical achievements has been shown by, for example, Aunola, Leskinen, Lerkkanen, and Nurmi (2004), Aunio and Niemivirta (2010), Jordan, Kaplan, Ramineni, and Locuniak (2009) as well as Hannula and Lehtinen (2001) and Hannula, Räsänen, and Lehtinen (2007). However, Hannula, Mattinen, and Lehtinen (2005) have also demonstrated that low-achieving children who take part in early childhood education (ECE) where an intense focus is directed to mathematical relationships and reasoning in routines and play can, over a relatively short period of time, enhance their conceptual understanding and reasoning skills. Further, the researchers show how these children can achieve as well as the majority of children even several years later.

Mathematical skills build to a large extent on the ability to reason logically about common relationships in space and time. Still, children are born into a world of mediating abstract symbols, principles and knowledge-specific meanings. Concepts and principles have been developed over thousands of years and get their meaning when individuals communicate with one another (Wittgenstein 1978). Social interaction and shared attention (Rogoff 1990; Rogoff 2003) therefore play an important role in the opportunities children are given to make use of mathematical symbols in communicating about how they experience relationships between objects encountered in everyday situations.

Mathematics education in early childhood

Comparative international studies (OECD 2001; OECD 2006; Dalli et al. 2011) show that children whose early learning takes place in high-quality educational milieus are more likely to develop their language and cognitive skills. A factor of critical importance for high-quality educational environments is the educators' willingness and ability to form relationships with children that will support learning and development.

A core principle in ECE is that education should be planned and conducted with sensitivity both to the experiences the children already have within a specific field of knowledge, and to the knowledge and issues that are in focus and under development (Clements 2004; Pramling Samuelsson and Asplund Carlsson 2008). Among the same group of children, there might be several different ways to understand the same concept (von Glasersfeld 1995). As children's different perspectives come up against culturally negotiated understandings, this sets demands on the educator's skills of interpreting the situation, embracing the children's perspectives, and then directing their attention to a more developed way of understanding the same concept. Communication and interaction are in this respect essential, in that children should be given opportunities to express their personal understanding and interpret others' ways of understanding (Rogoff 2003; Björklund 2010a). Griffin (2004) and Casey (2004) suggest that this has to be taken into consideration when planning for ECE, in that children with different entry-level knowledge will have the opportunity to learn something through communicating about a common issue in the different activities in which they engage.

Interaction, for example in children's play, is mostly characterised by meaningfulness and a common interest. Children's play is considered meaningful from the children's own perspectives. Early childhood educators can use this context to plan for learning where, whilst children's intentions and interests are taken into account, there is also a focus on themes and topics from the curriculum, as meaningful knowledge is always closely connected to practice and situated in context (Wittgenstein 1978; Lave and Wenger 1991).

Dowker (2005) describes mathematical development and understanding as a complex mixture of three knowledge domains. One is factual knowledge that includes memorised number facts such as, for example counting-rhymes, a common theme in many nursery rhymes. Another domain is procedural knowledge, which encompasses the child's knowing how to proceed in order to get an answer to a problem. The third domain, conceptual knowledge, is closely allied with the way in which a person might be described as 'good' at mathematics. Conceptual knowledge means that the person understands why a strategy works and why a certain procedure is more effective than another. In ECE it is this third domain that, according to Cross, Woods, and Schweingruber (2009), should be focused on, in that children will learn not only how to count and use instruments of measurement, but also how to reason about procedures and outcomes. One important role for the educator is therefore to support children in gaining mathematical insights in explorative play and in developing conceptual understanding in meaningful communicative situations (Griffin 2004; Buys and de Moor 2008).

Variation Theory of learning

Variation Theory of learning offers a framework for studies that analyse how learning is realised in education. To educate children in mathematics one has to focus not only on what is to be learnt, but also on how it is to be learnt and what it is actually possible to learn in any particular setting (Runesson 2005).

Every phenomenon that a person experiences is regarded as consisting of a number of aspects that are critical for a certain understanding to come about. Variation within and between aspects makes it possible for the individual to discern and experience the phenomenon in a particular way. For example the child cannot discern and explore relationships in space, number or magnitude if there is never more than one object present (Marton and Booth 1997; Runesson 1999; Runesson 2005). Nor is it possible to experience the abstraction of numbers if the child always encounters similar objects in groups that are to be counted. Educating children therefore involves bringing forth these aspects through variation and making it possible for children to discern and explore relationships in the aspects that are in the teacher's focus (Runesson and Marton 2002; Marton and Tsui 2004).

That which the educator intends the children to learn is called the object of learning. How the educator focuses attention on the aspects that are discernible in any given situation creates a space of learning. It is this space of learning that forms the central focus of Variation Theory of learning (Marton and Tsui 2004).

The educator's professional knowledge and skills may be described as the ability to plan learning objectives suitable for a specific group of children. A learning objective in ECE could be that the youngest children become acquainted with the concept of size and more specifically the relative meaning in verbal concepts that describe different types of size. To support the youngest children's development of the idea of size, the educator will herself need knowledge of the relativity in mathematical concepts that describe spatial relationships between objects. At the same time she (or he, but she in this study) also needs an idea of how to capture children's interest at any particular moment and how to arrange situations where learning and play can be combined as a means of exploring physical similarities and differences, such as size.

There are great opportunities to support children's developing understanding of concepts relating to spatial relationships since many of these aspects are naturally relevant in the play and games that children themselves initiate and engage in. All manner of different sorting games can work as the inspiration for comparing and contrasting similarities and differences in varying features, and in communicating with others about processes of exploration and the features that are discerned.

The project

If there is to be a reasonable possibility to discern what happens within a complex process such as education, the design of research studies assumes a crucial importance. Within the framework of Variation Theory of learning, so called Learning Studies are used to explore and develop teaching methods. Learning Studies aim to enhance educators' understanding of the object of learning as a means of developing effective ways to present critical features to their students (Marton and Tsui 2004).

The design chosen for the current study is inspired by the Learning Study design, but with great respect to the conditions of ECE where goals and educational methods differ from those in the compulsory school context. To date, only a handful of studies based on the idea and design of Learning Study have been carried out in pre-school education (Pramling and Pramling Samuelsson 2008; Björklund 2011). Thus there is a need to explore more thoroughly the design of Learning Studies in ECE settings.

The core of the Learning Study design is the teachers' process of scrutinising what is critical to discern in order to understand a specific phenomenon or concept. This is accomplished through reflective discussion with other teachers and/or a researcher and analysis of the intended object of learning and how this is experienced by the learner. The purpose is then to find effective strategies for education and to share reliable knowledge with other educators (Marton and Tsui 2004).

According to the Finnish curriculum for ECE (Stakes 2004), the child's learning should be seen as a whole, where thematic education is preferred and the focus is on each child's own intentions and interests. Whilst at first sight this might seem to be contrary to the Learning Study concept, the idea of learning and opportunities to discern critical aspects of a learning objective can in fact be beneficial in terms of developing the professionalism of educators in ECE. This is the main purpose for using the design in this study.

The Learning Study developed in this project involved a design for developing educators' awareness of mathematics and how it is experienced by the children they are working with. Within the context of the design, the educator's focus is directed to discerning critical aspects of a specific mathematical concept and children's understanding of the same concept.

The complexity of mathematical concepts is challenging not only for the child (Björklund 2007) but also for the educator, who needs to be very sensitive to the child's expressed understanding. To discover the extent and qualities of a child's conception of a particular concept, the educator has to have highly developed skills in interpreting children's actions as expressions of their understanding. A videographic approach may work as a base for reflection-on-action (Lindahl 2002; Björklund 2010b) and as a kind of self-evaluation (Rönnerman 2003) that can provide many important insights into what happens in an activity.

Four kindergarten teachers (each with qualifications in education) took part in the in-service program. These educators work with children in the 1–3-, 4–5- and 6-year-old age ranges in the day-care system in Finland. The educator working in the toddler group is the object of the analysis presented in this article.

Reflection-on-action is an important part of the program, as it provides the base for further planning. Planning takes place both beforehand, when deciding on materials and activities, and also in action. Reflection-in-action is one kind of reflection where intuition about how a situation can be interpreted as a whole impacts on the way that the practitioner acts (Schön 1991). When the educator senses that she and the child do not understand each other's intentions, she interprets this by 'reflecting-in-action' and adjusts either her own point of departure or aspects of the context so that the child can have better opportunities to explore and discern the intended object of learning.

The methodological purpose of the program is to enhance the educator's ability to reflect-in-action by means of videographic evaluation on-action and it is hoped that the effects of this will emerge in qualitatively improved interaction between adult and child. The educational quality and effects of the in-service program are analysed in a qualitative manner, where changes in the educator's strategies, utterances and actions are related to the children's continuing interest in an activity and to new initiatives that are taken.

Videographic data was collected during five learning sessions. The parents of the participating children provided their written consent. The participants' names have been changed so that recognition of individual children will not be possible. Each session generated approximately one hour of data and a total of seven toddlers participated in the activities. The learning objective determined by the educator was that the children should become acquainted with quantities by discerning and exploring relationships in size and the contrasting concepts 'small' and 'big'. Materials chosen by the educator were, in the first session, balls and cubes, and thereafter buttons, toy animals, play-dough and, in the final session, building blocks. The overall idea was to use materials that the children were already familiar with and that they had used previously for other purposes and in their play.

After each session the researcher and the educator evaluated the session together. This procedure strengthens the reliability of the analysis, as the participating educator and objective observer (the current researcher) analysed the same data material, adopting their own perspectives in generating a common understanding of the same situation. When all five learning sessions had been completed, an open in-depth interview was carried out as a conclusion of the program, the aim being to follow up the educator's experiences.

Results

The analysis of the educational work with mathematical concepts in toddler day-care shows how some aspects stand out as critical and as of particular relevance in the discussion of toddlers exploring mathematics. These essential aspects are the educator's *ability to discern opportunities for exploring mathematics, awareness articulated in action, nuances in the verbally expressed mathematics* and *taking the child's intentions as a starting point*. In the sections that follow each of these essential aspects is presented and discussed in turn.

Ability to discern opportunities for exploring mathematics

An enhanced awareness of the features of the object of learning can make the educator more sensitive to what the child says and the initiatives the child takes, when it comes to the chosen object of learning. Opportunities to problematise and elicit variation can present themselves in natural ways that the child can explore and learn from. The child experiences this heightened awareness in situations where the educator listens to the child and follows the intentions of the child:

Two children and the educator are sorting buttons. Anette (educator) has presented the buttons as different in sizes using the descriptive concepts 'small' and 'big'. Anette picks up three buttons, each of a different size, in her hand.

Rose (2:10) points at the smallest button: 'What is this called?'

Anette: 'What is it called? I think you know, we just talked about it'.

Rose: 'I don't know.'

Anette: 'If we think of big and small, what is it then?'

Rose: 'Small!'

Anette: 'Small, yes. Now, where is the big button? There!' as Rose points at the biggest button.

Rose gives Anette another small white button: 'Now you've got one more'.

Anette: 'Wow, what do these buttons look like?'

Rose picks on the two small white buttons in Anette's hand: 'Small'.

Anette: 'Small, are they exactly the same?'

Rose: 'Yes!'

The situation described above may not be unique or even uncommon in ECE. Nevertheless, it provides a good example of how to capture and direct a child's intentions, the importance of the educator knowing the complexity of the concepts being worked with, and how to enable critical aspects to be made visible for the child to discern. The idea is not to get the child to give a correct answer but, rather, to focus on and compare features of the buttons in the educator's hand. By giving the child contrasting alternatives, she is given an opportunity to reflect on similarities and differences. When the educator holds the buttons in her hand, it becomes clear where the focus is directed and this supports the child–adult interaction. Within these frames the child takes initiatives to further explore the concepts, as she offers a second small button to the educator. In the educator's palm is thus constituted the essence of Variation Theory, in that variation both between concepts and within concepts is discernible.

From the data collected, one can only interpret tendencies to progress in understanding in the sense that the children seem to act in a different way. The educator expresses her own heightened awareness of how the children take initiatives to use mathematical concepts in spontaneous situations during the day, for example indoors as well as outdoors, in the hallway, the toilet or the playroom. The educator seems to observe an increased awareness of mathematics in the children's spontaneous utterances and initiatives that will give them greater opportunities to explore concepts and to test their own understanding in relation to others'. At the same time, this may be caused by *her own* increased awareness of the opportunities to explore mathematics in daily activities and, in so doing, support the children's initiatives in a different way than before. From these data, it is not possible to analyse this relationship in a reliable way, but, taking the child's perspective, the effect is probably the same; as the educator's awareness of mathematics is enhanced, the children are given more opportunities to explore and communicate mathematics.

Awareness articulated in action

The interaction between educator and children shows that the educator finds new ways of drawing the children's attention to a specified object of learning. At the same time she shows sensitivity to the child's interests, perspectives and understanding.

In the second learning session the educator planned an activity that would direct focus not just on the concepts 'big' and 'small', but also 'middle-sized'. She knows, from her earlier experiences, that buttons fascinated the children, but they have not previously worked with buttons as a means of challenging the meaning of mathematical concepts. The children have some difficulties in selecting 'a big button', and the educator reflects on this:

> Maybe it was a bit too diffuse with the idea of sizes, to see the buttons. Maybe it was too hard for them.

The educator attempts to discriminate the meaning of the concepts big and small by giving the children an opportunity to sort buttons. Two girls are given a tray each, on which they start to scoop the buttons from a big box. When they have filled their trays the educator asks them to sort their buttons. The girls do not show any initiative in sorting the buttons, but pick around on the trays, showing the buttons they find interesting to the educator. The educator then asks if the button is big or small. It is worth noting that the question has no fixed answer, since the button may very well be described as either big or small depending on the other buttons it is compared with:

> Rose (2:10): 'Small'
> Anette: 'You think it is small. If you look at this button then, what do you think this is?', pointing at a smaller button among the other buttons on the tray.
> Rose: 'Small'.
> Anette: 'What is this button then?', pointing at the first button.
> Rose: 'Big'.

The child is here given an opportunity to experience one of the most essential aspects of understanding the concept of size; that size is relative and depends on the other objects involved in the comparison. A small button is only small compared with a bigger one, as the big button may very well be considered small in comparison with an even bigger one. However, in the sorting activity it seems to be difficult for the children to explore the complex meaning of the concepts, initiating a strategy switch on the part of the educator as she demarcates two particular buttons. This enables the child to compare and discern similarities and differences, thus making comparison possible even for a two-year-old.

Nuances in the verbally expressed mathematics

Verbal concepts are important when exploring mathematical relationships since they enable differentiation of the experienced relationship between two objects. Two toy animals or buttons may very well be considered 'small' but, provided they are not exactly the same size, when compared with one another, one is bigger than the other. By picking up on the initiative of one of the children to compare and focus on similarities in sizes, the child in the next example is given great opportunities to explore the meaning of the concepts:

> Anette places two buttons in her hand that Allie (2:11) considered as being 'big'. Anette then asks, 'Do they look the same? Are they equally big?'

In this short exchange two important aspects are introduced to the child. First, the more general question is whether the buttons look the same. They may very well differ in many ways, for example in shape, colour and size. Second, attention is focused on a specific feature, namely size. When two buttons are placed side by side, it is possible for the child to demonstrate her awareness of aspects of the specific learning objective. On the tray with hundreds of buttons of all different shapes, colours and sizes, it becomes very difficult to discern certain features and compare all the buttons. Comparison thus becomes a simultaneous focus on two objects, taking into consideration their similarities and differences. The more objects that are compared, the more difficult the task is.

Familiarity in meaning seems to be of importance for the toddlers in the sorting tasks. In the third learning session, in which toy animals were introduced to the children in a large box, the toddlers had no difficulties in sorting them into collections and series of sizes. Many of the toddlers used the familiar concepts of 'mother', 'father' and 'baby' to discriminate sizes within a collection or 'family' of the same kind of animals. After sorting the toys first into families, they showed no problems in using the mathematical terms 'small', 'the smallest', 'middle-sized', 'big' and 'the biggest'.

Taking the child's intentions as a starting point

Even if the material used in the learning session and the learning objective is determined in advance, the educator gives the children fairly loose boundaries, in that they can explore the materials in their own ways. Most children seem eager to play with and explore the materials given to them and the educator is thus given an opportunity to interpret the children's previous experiences and current understanding, a necessity in terms of finding ways for the children to explore the meaning of specific concepts.

The educator lets the children take their time, but asks them questions, partly as a means of getting an understanding of their intentions, and partly to challenge their understanding. This later part is also a challenge for the educator who has to capture the child's interest at a particular moment in time and, thereafter, to try and direct the child's attention to a certain aspect of the object of learning. However, when this is accomplished it stimulates the child's interest in the activity and seems to trigger the child's own curiosity and reflection on the commonly focused objective. An interest in the child's intention is a key to learning as variations of critical aspects are then given attention in a meaningful and natural way:

> Anette (educator) sits down beside Albin (2:10) who is sorting blocks and balls.
> Anette: 'That's very nice, how many do you have, Albin?'
> Albin: 'This many'. Albin continues sorting.
> Anette: 'Shall we count? How many are there? I will help you count, what do we start with? One, and then two and then three' and points at one ball at a time.
> Albin: 'No' and looks in another direction.

Anette: 'How many small balls do you have? One small.' At the same time Albin points at a ball at the bottom of a cup.

Anette: 'What do you call these?' and points at one of two larger oval blocks.

Albin looks at the oval blocks: 'A barrel'.

Anette: 'Yes, it looks like a barrel, that is the yellow barrel, where do you want to put this funny barrel? Do you think there are any more barrels?'

Albin: 'Yes' and puts the yellow block in another cup.

Anette: 'Shall we look for some?'

Albin rapidly picks up a black ball: 'Black!'

Anette: 'Black, is it a barrel that one?'

Albin: 'No, round' and shows it to Anette, 'Ball'.

Anette: 'Are there any more funny barrels?'

Albin looks intensely into the box with blocks and balls and picks up a small block: 'Here is one'.

Anette: 'There is one, what is it called?'

Albin: 'Small'.

Anette: 'Do you mean a small barrel?'

Albin: 'Yes' and places the block in an upright position and says 'it can stand up'.

Anette: 'Can we compare them, Albin, look, what is the difference?' and takes the big yellow barrel from the cup and puts it standing besides the black barrel at the table.

Albin looks closely at the two barrels, takes the smaller one and places it on top of the bigger one. The blocks have holes going right through them.

Anette: 'Yes, has it [the smaller block] room inside it [the bigger block]?'

Albin tries to put the smaller block inside the bigger one from both ends but with no success, 'No', he places the big yellow block to stand again and the black one on top of it.

Anette: 'Can you find any more big barrels?'

Albin searches in the box and picks up another small black barrel. He holds the two black ones next to each other.

Anette: 'Are they exactly the same?'

Albin: 'Yes, they are'.

Anette: 'Can you find a big barrel?' Albin hesitates, 'It can be in another colour as well'.

Albin then rapidly picks out an orange barrel, 'This one'.

Anette: 'Good, yes'.

Here the educator pays attention to what the child finds interesting and tries to find out what he is willing to participate in and communicate about. His rapid response 'no' to the counting suggestion indicates that he will not take part in any counting activities, which makes the educator change her strategy, focusing on shape and colour instead. These features are, it would seem, more familiar to the child and he is eager to find more and compare them with one another. The educator is still highly sensitive to his response, keeping the idea of problematising concepts of big and small in mind, but shaping the activity so that he will be able to explore the meaning of the concepts on his own terms. This example highlights the idea that, if they are to find a common starting point and together explore the meaning of concepts, it is critical to be precise as to which feature the educator and child are talking about.

Conclusions

The analysis of the strategies for enhancing children's opportunities to explore mathematical concepts in this educational program clearly indicates the importance of discernment and awareness. Awareness is a factor that cannot be overstated when it comes to ECE in general and toddlers' exploration of mathematics in particular. Through the Learning Study design, the educator is given an opportunity to focus on one aspect of mathematics at a time, in this case the concept of size. This gives her a frame for exploring how the concept is realised by the toddlers and the ways that seem to enable her to reach out to the children and support their developing understanding. Awareness of the content itself is not enough; this study shows the necessity of integrating an enhanced awareness into practice, in terms of discerning mathematics by taking the child's perspective, catching the children's intentions, and realising how verbal expressions may be interpreted by the children.

Mathematical understanding and use includes a complex cognitive skill that develops during the childhood years. Spontaneous recognition and experimentation with mathematical concepts, principles and ideas are extremely important for further learning. However, there are indications that not all children focus spontaneously on mathematical relationships (Hannula et al. 2005). Because of this, it is important that children even younger than the age of three encounter educators who can support their developing awareness of mathematical relationships in daily routines and play. The Learning Study design seems to increase the educators' awareness of mathematical ideas and how children are able to discern and explore them in well-known and meaningful situations.

For one of the children described in this article, Albin, it is important to meet an educator who has this sensitivity and the skill to capture his attention because he does not yet understand some aspects of the phenomenon in question or does not have any interest in it, and will probably not ask about it. This particular child will therefore not challenge himself in areas where he does not feel comfortable, such as counting and using number words. Taking another approach, in this case his interest in comparing shapes and different colours, can support his basic understanding of relations between the different features of the objects in focus. With a solid basic understanding he can find interest in, and build up his confidence to explore, other mathematical relationships, such as numbers. This has also been shown to be an effective approach in studies with older children (Björklund 2011).

The analysis of the educator's educational approach shows that children also experience heightened awareness in the way that the educator listens to the child and follows the child's intentions. This seems to further strengthen the child's concentration and the length of the time that the child can hold on to the same idea, as described in the episode with Albin. It is important to find strategies that will keep focus on an intended object of learning, as here for example in comparing a collection of buttons that, although they may vary in several features, have some in common, as the simultaneity in reflection on aspects of the object of learning is essential in order for a more developed understanding to take form.

It is sometimes necessary to sharply demarcate specific features, concepts or phenomena from the general surroundings in order for the child to be able to focus on critical aspects. Indeed simplifying or 'marking off' may be the key to realising mathematical relationships as has been shown in recent studies in the same project (Björklund 2011). Observations from this study provide convincing support for this idea in that this sort of demarcating can function as an effective way of guiding the toddler's attention to a specific focal phenomenon.

Space of learning is constituted by a common focus. If educator and child do not meet each other on an intellectual level or have a common point of departure in their communication, supporting learning and development may be difficult. Recent research on mathematics education (Kilhamn 2011) has demonstrated the necessity of using adequate language in the teaching of new as well as previously encountered concepts. Lacking the basic knowledge of a certain concept leads to difficulties in interpreting what the educator says and in understanding the metaphors that are used. It is thus important that, on the one hand, children are given opportunities to learn to understand the basics of mathematics in meaningful and concrete situations and, on the other, that educators are aware of the importance of using suitable language and listening to how the children use newly introduced concepts. The ways in which children respond to and use concepts can tell us a lot about their interpretations and understandings.

According to the Finnish national curriculum for ECE (Stakes 2004) as well as recent research on children's learning in the early years, education should include taking the child's perspective and intentions into consideration at the same time as the educator has a specific learning objective in focus. However, working in this way sets demands on the educator's ability to capture the child's interest and skills and to direct the child's attention to certain aspects of the intended object of learning. In order to accomplish this, Löwing (2004) argues that the educator has to have a theoretical knowledge of how to teach and learn the subject in question. This means that the educator has reflected upon what it means to understand something, how children learn about this and how to make it possible to learn it. Working with a Variation Theory approach, where both the educator and the child can be recognised as learners, and using Learning Study as part of a program for professional development may be one way of exploring these necessities.

References

Aunio, P., and M. Niemivirta. 2010. Predicting children's mathematical performance in grade one by early numeracy. *Learning and Individual Differences* 20: 427–35.

Aunola, K., E. Leskinen, M.-K. Lerkkanen, and J.-E. Nurmi. 2004. Developmental dynamics of math performance from preschool to grade 2. *Journal of Educational Psychology* 96, no. 4: 699–713.

Björklund, C. 2007. *Hållpunkter för lärande. Småbarns möten med matematik* [Critical conditions of learning: Toddlers encountering mathematics, in Swedish]. PhD diss., Åbo Akademi University.

Björklund, C. 2010a. Broadening the horizon: Toddlers' strategies for learning mathematics. *International Journal of Early Years Education* 18, no. 1: 71–84.

Björklund, C. 2010b. Att fånga komplexiteten i små barns lärande – en metodologisk reflektion [Capturing the complexity in toddlers' learning process - a methodological reflection, in Swedish]. *Nordisk Barnehageforskning* 3, no. 1: 111–20.

Björklund, C. 2011. One step back, two steps forward: An educator's experiences from a learning study of basic mathematics in preschool special education. *Scandinavian Journal of Eductional Research*, iFirst Article: 1–21.

Buys, K., and E. de Moor. 2008. Domain description measurement. In *Young children learn measurement and geometry: A learning-teaching trajectory with intermediate attainment targets for the lower grades in primary school*, ed. Marja van den Heuvel-Panhuizen and Kees Buys, 15–36. Rotterdam: Sense Publishers.

Casey, B. 2004. Mathematics problem-solving adventures: A language-arts-based supplementary series for early childhood that focuses on spatial sense. In *Engaging young children in mathematics: Standards for early childhood mathematics education*, ed. Douglas Clements, Julie Sarama, and Ann-Marie DiBiase, 377–90. Mahwah, NJ: Lawrence Erlbaum.

Clements, D. 2004. Major themes and recommendations. In *Engaging young children in mathematics: Standards for early childhood mathematics education*, ed. D. Clements, J. Sarama, and A.-M. DiBiase, 7–76. Mahwah, NJ: Lawrence Erlbaum.

Cross, C., T. Woods, and H. Schweingruber. 2009. *Mathematics learning in early childhood: Paths towards excellence and equity*. Washington, DC: National Academies Press.

Dalli, C., E.J. White, J. Rockel, I. Duhn, with E. Buchanan, S. Davidson, S. Ganly, L. Kus, and B. Wang. 2011. *Quality early childhood education for under-two-year-olds: What should it look like? A literature review*. Ministry of Education New Zealand.

Doverborg, E., and I. Pramling Samuelsson. 2004. Varför skall barn inte märka att de lär sig matematik? *Nämnaren* 3: 2–4.

Dowker, A. 2005. *Individual differences in arithmetic: Implications for psychology, neuroscience and education*. New York: Psychology Press.

Griffin, S. 2004. Number worlds: A research-based mathematics program for young children. In *Engaging young children in mathematics: Standards for early childhood mathematics education*, ed. D. Clements, J. Sarama, and A.-M. DiBiase, 325–42. Mahwah, NJ: Lawrence Erlbaum.

Hannula, M., and E. Lehtinen. 2001. Spontaneous tendency to focus on numerosities in the development of cardinality. In *Proceedings of the 25th Conference of the International Group for the Psychology of Mathematics Education*, ed. Marja van den Heuvel-Panhuizen, 113–20. The Netherlands: Amersfoort Drukkerij Wilco.

Hannula, M., A. Mattinen, and E. Lehtinen. 2005. Does social interaction influence 3-year-old children's tendency to focus on numerosity? A quasi-experimental study in day-care. In *Learning environments to promote deep conceptual and strategic learning*, ed. L. Verschaffel, E. de Corte, G. Kanselaar, and M. Valcke, 63–80. Studia Paedagogica, Leuven: Leuven University Press.

Hannula, M., P. Räsänen, and E. Lehtinen. 2007. Development of counting skills: Role of spontaneous focusing on numerosity and subitizing-based enumeration. *Mathematical Thinking and Learning* 9, no. 1: 51–7.

Jordan, N., D. Kaplan, C. Ramineni, and M. Locuniak. 2009. Early math matters: Kindergarten number competence and later mathematics outcome. *Developmental Psychology* 45, no. 3: 850–67.

Kilhamn, C. 2011. Making sense of negative numbers. PhD diss., University of Gothenburg.

Lave, J., and E. Wenger. 1991. *Situated learning: Legitimate peripheral participation*. Cambridge: Cambridge University Press.

Levine, S., L. Whealton Suriyakham, M.L. Rowe, J. Huttenlocher, and E.A. Gunderson. 2010. What counts in the development of young children's number knowledge? *Developmental Psychology* 46, no. 5: 1309–19.

Lindahl, M. 2002. *Vårda–vägleda–lära. Effektstudie av ett interventionsprogram för pedagogers lärande i förskolemiljön* [Caring–guiding–learning. Effect study of an intervention program for educators' learning in a pre-school environment, in Swedish]. Göteborg: Acta Universitatis Gothoburgensis.

Löwing, M. 2004. Matematikundervisningens konkreta gestaltning. En studie av kommunikationen lärare-elev och matematiklektionens didaktiska ramar [A concrete formation of mathematics teaching. A study of communication between teachers and pupils and the educational framework of mathematical classrooms, in Swedish]. PhD diss., University of Gothenburg.

Marton, F., and S. Booth. 1997. *Learning and awareness*. Mahwah, NJ: Lawrence Erlbaum.

Marton, F., and A. Tsui, eds. 2004. *Classroom discourse and the space of learning*. Mahwah, NJ: Lawrence Erlbaum.

McCrink, K., and K. Wynn. 2004. Large-number addition and subtraction by 9-month-old infants. *Psychological Science* 15, no. 11: 776–81.

OECD. 2001. *Starting Strong I.* Paris: OECD Publishing.

OECD. 2006. *Starting Strong II.* Paris: OECD Publishing.

Pramling, N., and I. Pramling Samuelsson, eds. 2008. *Didaktiska studier från förskola och skola* [Didactical studies from pre-school and school, in Swedish]. Malmö: Gleerups.

Pramling Samuelsson, I., and M. Asplund Carlsson. 2008. The playing learning child: Towards a pedagogy of early childhood. *Scandinavian Journal of Educational Research* 52, no. 6: 623–41.

Rogoff, B. 1990. *Apprenticeship in thinking: Cognitive development in social context.* New York: Oxford University Press.

Rogoff, B. 2003. *The cultural nature of human development.* Cary, NC: Oxford University Press.

Runesson, U. 1999. *Variationens pedagogik. Skilda sätt att behandla ett matematiskt innehåll* [The pedagogy of variations. Different ways of handling a mathematical topic, in Swedish]. PhD diss., University of Gothenburg.

Runesson, U. 2005. Beyond discourse and interaction. Variation: A critical aspect for teaching and learning mathematics. *Cambridge Journal of Education* 35, no. 1: 69–87.

Runesson, U., and F. Marton. 2002. The object of learning and the space of variation. In *What matters? Discovering critical conditions of classroom learning,* ed. F. Marton and P. Morris. Göteborg: Acta Universitatis Gothoburgensis.

Rönnerman, K. 2003. Action research: Educational tools and the improvement of practice. *Educational Action Research* 11, no. 1: 9–21.

Schön, D. 1991. *The reflective practitioner: How professionals think in action.* Avebury, Aldershot: Ashgate.

Siegler, R., and G. Ramani. 2009. Playing linear number board games – but not circular ones – improves low-income preschoolers' numerical understanding. *Journal of Educational Psychology* 101, no. 3: 545–60.

Stakes 2004. *National Curriculum Guidelines on Early Childhood Education and Care in Finland (ECEC).* National Institute for Health and Welfare (THL). http://varttua.stakes.fi/NR/rdonlyres/78BC5411-F37C-494C-86FA-BE40929 4709B/0/e_vasu.pdf (accessed February 17, 2010).

Von Glasersfeld, E. 1995. *Radical constructivism: A way of knowing and learning.* London: Falmer Press.

Wittgenstein, L. 1978. *Remarks on the foundations of mathematics.* London: MIT Press.

Wynn, K. 1998. Numerical competence in infants. In *The development of mathematical skills,* ed. C. Donlan, 3–25. Hove: Psychology Press.

'Wasted down there': policy and practice with the under-threes

Rory McDowall Clark and Sue Baylis

Institute of Education, University of Worcester, Worcester, UK

Although frameworks now exist for quality provision for under-threes, discourses underpinning policy remain conflicted. The split between care and education is still firmly entrenched in provision and a gap remains between rhetoric and practice. This paper explores how Early Years Professional Status, which requires practitioners to engage meaningfully with babies and toddlers, can support the development of 'thoughtful agents' as shared learning enables new insights and understanding to emerge. In particular it offers a context which transforms practitioners' sense of themselves as professionals and provides opportunities for child-centred practice to exert an upward influence. The theoretical basis for this paper is the concept of learning communities whereby EYPS becomes a cultural 'tool' and the means by which learning is mediated. Conclusions are that experience with infants empowers practitioners to engage in the high-level critical reflection necessary to challenge political prescription and an emphasis on early years as preparation for school.

Introduction

In the twenty-first century Early Childhood Education and Care (ECEC) has moved beyond the province of practitioners and academics to become a focus for those who had previously shown little interest in the field such as politicians, economists and the business sector. The extent of this raised profile is such that Woodhead (2009) suggests early childhood is now a 'global phenomenon'. Increased investment and attention stem from recognition of the dual role that ECEC plays within a neo-liberal economy; it not only pays educational dividends in an increasingly competitive, globalised economy but also enables parents (and mothers in particular) to seek employment and thus ease the burden on state spending (McDowall Clark 2011). We would argue that the resulting tensions and contradictions for ECEC have particular implications for policy and provision for under-threes and the practitioners working with them.

Background context

In the UK the past decade has seen a huge increase in policies relating to the early years. Curriculum reform alongside greater emphasis on professional development of staff would seem to bode well for realisation of the sort of vision the sector has long argued for (e.g. Pugh 1988; Moss and Penn 1996). In England concerted action under the previous government to rationalise a patchwork of provision, qualifications and governance culminated in the Childcare Act of 2006 which set the context for a foundation stage curriculum covering birth to five (DCSF 2008) to be led by graduate pedagogues (Early Years Professionals, or EYPs). Funding amounting to more than £550 million was made available under the Transformation Fund (TF) and later the Graduate Leader Fund (GLF) to support the development of graduate practitioners in the private, voluntary and independent sectors (Mathers et al. 2011). These measures sent a clear signal that coherence as well as the quality of provision was important and indicate some grounds for the optimism displayed by Nutbrown and Page (2009) who, recognising that work with children under three has usually been regarded as 'relatively unimportant', suggest:

> But things are different now … politicians can no longer be accused of behaving as if, in education terms at least, life begins at five years of age. Babies and toddlers are now firmly fixed in the education and care agenda of government in the UK and other countries around the world and issues relating to the quality of provision made for them are central to policy. (2009, 8)

However, this new focus on babies and toddlers has always been underpinned by a variety of contradictory agendas with the result that, although the frameworks are now in place to develop high quality provision for the under-threes, the discourses which inform this remain conflicted. Encouragement for growth within the childcare sector under the previous government was primarily driven by the hope that parents would be encouraged off benefits and into employment (Baldock 2011). A new government took office in the UK in May 2010 but this is likely to remain the foremost official perception of provision for the under-threes despite a strong rationale supporting appropriately holistic provision for babies and toddlers in the recent review of the Early Years Foundation Stage (Tickell 2011). Recent policy direction in respect of young children has been informed by the coalition government's response to the Field Report into poverty (Field 2010), the Allen Report on early intervention (Allen 2011) and the Tickell Review of the EYFS (Tickell 2011). As a result continued investment is planned to support targeted family-based early intervention to enable children from disadvantaged backgrounds to catch up with their peers (Teather 2011).

Baldock recognises that public understanding is frequently behind that of experts in the field when he suggests that 'There is still considerable reluctance outside the early years profession to accept the kind of understanding of child development that is common among practitioners' (2011, 125). We would contend that this is particularly the case in respect of work with babies, and that moreover this persists within the profession itself where working with pre-school children is still, perhaps unconsciously, perceived as more important and requiring a higher calibre of staff. Such attitudes need to be addressed before the potential of graduate leadership of the sector can be fully realised. This paper debates the rhetoric and reality of working with infants and explores the opportunities for reflective practice and professional growth as a result of a learning-community approach (Lave and Wenger 1991) to gaining Early Years Professional Status.

The professionalism of care

Although there are some indications that the persistent split between care and education (Bennett 2003) is becoming less pronounced, it is a division that is still firmly entrenched in connection with provision for the youngest children. The Childcare Act (DfES 2006) officially abolished this distinction but historically practitioners working with this age group have been viewed as caregivers rather than educators and this division has not only downplayed the professionalism of care (Taggart 2011) but also served to reinforce the lower status they are so frequently afforded (Manning-Morton 2006).

Two key factors undervalue work with babies and toddlers; first the persistent dominance of the maternal discourse (Ailwood 2008), which characterises skill and proficiency as 'natural' and 'innate' attributes, and second the emotional connection to young children that is such a key aspect of the role (Elfer, Goldschmied, and Selleck 2003; Petrie and Owen 2006). The maternal discourse stems from a view of childcare as providing a substitute mother role, a gendered image that assumes:

> ... little or no education is necessary to undertake the work, which is understood as requiring qualities or competencies that are either innate to women ('maternal instinct') or else acquired through women's practice of domestic labour ('housework skills'). (Moss 2006, 34)

The enduring legacy of Bowlby (1953) is evident here in an emphasis on the primary importance of reciprocal, 'bonding' relationships between babies and their adult caregivers; this view underpins the contemporary practice of key workers but can also serve to make their role seem something less than professional.

Moyles (2001) has challenged the 'paradox of passion' whereby emotional responses to young children, vital to fulfilling a practitioner's role, may also restrict early years practice to a 'low-level operation in which children receive care but which negates or rejects education' (2001, 82). The affective aspects of the role are increasingly recognised as an essential feature of professionalism (e.g. Osgood 2010a; Osgood 2010b); however, a major contributing factor to low status remains the strongly gendered nature of the workforce. This has prompted Taggart (2011) to challenge 'the outdated equation between caring and female irrationality or anti-intellectualism', arguing that the 'moral seriousness' of work with young children needs to be seen as 'a central plank of professionalism' (2011, 85).

Despite this groundswell of growing respect for professionals working with babies and toddlers, because graduate-level practitioners have not been the norm in the UK as they are in many other countries, the perception remains that for maximum 'value' their skills and ability should be focused on preschool children. The recent evaluation of the GLF suggests there is little evidence that EYPs improved the quality of provision for children from birth to 30 months (Mathers et al. 2011). However, the authors also acknowledge that the low numbers of EYPs working with the younger children mean it is not possible to draw conclusions about their potential impact. Findings from other countries also support the fact that settings for infants and toddlers are less likely to be graduate led (Mathers et al. 2011) but such an attitude fails to recognise the professional expertise needed to 'create and sustain democratic encounters with children *from babyhood onwards*' (Pascal and Bertram 2009, 258, emphasis added) and that very particular skills are needed to work respectfully with infants. The undervaluing of those who work with this age group is a historical remnant of the undervaluing of babies themselves.

Changing views on babies

Babies were objects of official concern long before the under-fives became a focus for educational intervention; for instance in Britain the Infant and Life Protection Act of 1872, although 'a fairly feeble piece of legislation' (Baldock 2011), attempted some form of regulation of those caring for children under one year old. The fact that responsibility for this lay with medical officers of health is symptomatic of the 'health of the nation' ideology which has historically underpinned the governance of infants. Although, in much of the world, concern for babies is no longer rooted in fear for their physical survival, the vestiges of an approach based on feeding, changing and sleeping routines are still very much in evidence.

The traditional view of infants as primarily recipients of physical care stems from an understanding of them as incapable, powerless and fully dependent on adult caretakers (Canella 1997). This discourse of helplessness reinforces unequal power relationships which silence the child's voice and deny him/her agency. Such a limiting perception of young children, and the curtailment to their learning which it represents, has been challenged in recent years by a rights-based ethos which respects children as 'already social actors, not beings in the process of becoming such' (James and Prout 1997, vii). This offers an alternative perspective that recognises babies as powerful social beings and leads to very different adult–child relationships.

Recognition of babies as social beings supports a much more constructive approach to practice, which respects their significant capacities rather than emphasising what they are unable to do. Relationships and a pedagogy of listening (Rinaldi 1993) are fundamental and build on a respect for babies which recognises both their remarkable thinking abilities and also the necessity of encounters with other minds to support this development (Gopnik, Meltzoff, and Kuhl 1999). Interaction with others not only generates restructuring of the brain and supports a babies developing 'theory of mind' but also promotes their communicative abilities through co-regulation between babies and their adult caregivers (Trevarthen 1993). In drawing attention to the importance of 'protoconversations' with preverbal children Trevarthen emphasised the sensitivity required to respond when babies initiate communication. There is no doubt that babies are skilful communicators, but adults often fail to 'hear' what they have to say (Lancaster and Broadbent 2003) because of assumptions about the incompetence of infants.

As the first official guidance in Britain for working with babies and toddlers to go beyond basic care and welfare requirements, Birth to Three Matters (SureStart 2003) was grounded in a respect for young children's capabilities that had been evident in the literature for some time (e.g. Abbott and Moylett 1997; Goldschmied and Jackson 1994). The framework, with its focus on four aspects – a strong child, a skilful communicator, a competent learner and a healthy child – was warmly received by practitioners despite some initial concerns (particularly in the tabloid press) about a 'curriculum for babies'. Broad categories of development (such as 'Heads Up, Lookers and Communicators'), although perhaps rather cumbersome constructs, had the benefit of being more inclusive than an age-and-stage view of children's development. Although Birth to Three Matters had no statutory status, the influence of an approach based on principles rather than outcomes can be discerned in the themes and principles of the EYFS, published a few years later. In this way it can be considered as a rare example of a bottom-up rather than a top-down impetus. Furthermore, by incorporating the regulatory welfare requirements, the EYFS continued to erode traditional distinctions between care and education from birth onwards.

Official recognition of appropriate provision for the youngest children must be welcomed; but although policy is now in place in the UK to support holistic approaches with under-threes, within some sections of provision mindsets have yet to move on to meet it. A large gap remains between rhetoric and practice and this is particularly evident within the private, voluntary and independent (PVI) sector where the percentage of graduate practitioners is much lower than in maintained settings (Baldock, Fitzgerald, and Kay 2009).

Turning rhetoric into reality

The first part of this paper has traced the development of the current situation in England where a broad and holistic curriculum now exists for young children from birth onwards, supported by graduate EYPs, a 'role [which] will contribute to a new professional identity for the early years workforce' (Miller 2008, 256). We have argued that in respect of babies and toddlers a rhetorical gap persists between policy and practice as a result of the legacy of discourses of care. The rest of this paper sets out how the process of gaining EYPS has supported the professional development of practitioners, particularly in respect of under-threes, and argues the importance of hands-on experience with the youngest children to challenge practitioners' understandings of themselves as professionals.

If we are to bridge the rhetorical gap then this requires that practitioners become 'thoughtful agents' (Appleby and Andrews 2011, 59) who both reflect on and seek to improve provision. Such a role is envisaged for EYPs and is evident in the expectation that they should lead and model good practice. Both the Graduate and Undergraduate Practitioner pathways (previously known as Short Extended and Long Extended pathways) enable experienced practitioners to build on their knowledge and skills to gain professional status and this shared enterprise offers an encouraging environment which can support the development of 'a professional culture' (Anning and Edwards 2006). In this way EYPS itself becomes a cultural 'tool', the means by which learning is mediated (Engeström 1999) through dialogic interaction.

Our own EYPS provision is located within a Centre for Early Childhood which provides a range of undergraduate and postgraduate programmes across a broad community, including delivery within Children's Centres. From this perspective, learning is conceptualised as a social rather than an individual activity, an approach informed by the work of Lave and Wenger (Lave and Wenger 1991; Chaiklin and Lave 1993; Wenger 1998). This approach is particularly suited to EYPS where, rather than an individual cognitive pursuit, learning is fundamentally concerned with participating in practice (Wenger 1998). The following sections illustrate the way in which EYP candidates' ideas, values and working practices were informed and challenged by exploration of work with babies and toddlers.

Voices from the field

In order to successfully achieve EYP status candidates must be able to demonstrate not only knowledge and understanding but also the ability to lead practice across the whole of the EYFS age group from babyhood upwards. The main reason for candidates undertaking the short extended pathway has usually been that they lack experience with babies and toddlers. Those taking the long extended pathway already have foundation degrees and undertake EYPS whilst completing their full honours degree; these candidates come from a range of settings but significant numbers also lack experience with under-twos.

The participants whose experiences inform this paper were all female and ranged in age from their mid-twenties to early fifties. All are experienced practitioners working across a range of settings including kindergartens, nursery schools, private nurseries, pre-school playgroups and children's centres. Posts held included manager, deputy, room leader, early years adviser, children's centre teacher and a number of generic practitioners. This rich diversity of experience contributes to a dynamic professional dialogue through which learning is mediated.

Becoming 'thoughtful agents'

Many factors play a role in how people learn but Cole, Engeström, and Vasquez (1997) suggest that the most significant of these is the context in which learning takes place. This is sometimes referred to as 'situated learning' but the concept involves much more than the straightforward 'environment' or 'circumstances' in which learning takes place. Lave and Wenger (1991) suggest that situated learning goes beyond being located in time and space and is an integral constituent of social practice. The cultural and social practices which learners participate in therefore constitute a set of relations among people, their activity and the wider world 'over time and in relation with other tangential and overlapping communities of practice' (Lave and Wenger 1991, 98). It is these tangential and overlapping communities of practice which are integral to EYPs becoming 'thoughtful agents'. As practitioners in their own settings as well as participants in university programmes, prospective EYPs belong to a range of potential communities of practice; however these can only be effective if they have a shared focus and purpose. Wenger (1998) stresses the importance of:

> ... sustaining enough mutual engagement in pursuing an enterprise together to share some significant learning [so that] communities of practice can be thought of as shared histories of learning. (Wenger 1998, 86)

It is important to recognise that the concept of communities of practice arises from a social theory of learning rather than being a 'model' or 'method' for educational practice (Lave cited in Lea and Nicoll 2002). As such it provides a useful tool for examining the way that membership of a community of practice focusing on leadership of practice (see McDowall Clark and Baylis 2011) enabled many insights and new understandings of what it means to work with babies and toddlers to emerge.

Our role as providers was to encourage practitioners to reflect on and share thoughts about practice. Whilst it is important to encourage participants to apply their thinking across the EYFS age range we believed that the main focus should be on their roles as leaders of practice. However, learning 'belongs' to the group and each participant contributes and takes from the group according to her/his own needs and interests. As tutors it began to be apparent that much of the *new* learning, as opposed to simple sharing and affirmation of practice, arose as a result of either experience with, or discussion of, working with under-threes.

Emerging insights and understandings

Reflective practice is a 'complex, multi-faceted process which in its most effective form is personalised and owned by practitioners' (Appleby and Andrews 2011, 57). Therefore learning cannot be predetermined by the providers but an environment must be created whereby practitioners can extend their thinking and understanding and enhance their sense of the possible. Such an approach enables practitioners to make their tacit knowledge explicit and offers the potential to transform practice. In this way learning becomes a collective human activity (Cole and Engeström 1999) which opens up possibilities, rather than simply the transmission of information that potential EYP candidates had expected. Appleby and Andrews's (2011) model of reflective activity as a 'weave', representing the interrelation of the individual and the context, is a useful concept here. Candidates brought with them their own experiences and preconceptions of working with younger children and using 'threads' from others were enabled to create their own 'woven mat' of self-knowledge and professional identity. Journaling, reflective exercises and group-based analysis support this socio-cultural learning activity (Engeström 1999) and extracts from all of these discourses inform the following discussion.

Certain 'threads' and themes became particularly apparent through this process and whilst no claims are made about systematic collection of data or methodological rigour, this has enabled us to make a number of observations which we believe have wider applicability to the sector in general. Responses gathered from individual written accounts and from observations made in group discussions articulate the following themes.

Status and lack of visibility

There can sometimes be an assumption amongst those who have not themselves worked with babies that there cannot be much to it and that such work does not compare to the more demanding role of work with older children. The lower status of those who 'care' for the youngest children (Manning-Morton 2006) is perceptible within the profession as well as outside it, probably because in the past practitioners have not needed to confront these unthinking prejudices. The process of gaining EYPS requires meaningful involvement with babies and toddlers and so forces candidates to address assumptions which are then challenged by their own experience. They gain a new respect for the specific skills and abilities of those working with this age group, recognising the professionalism inherent in the role. This is also important for candidates whose usual working role is with the younger children, because the support of colleagues can help them to maintain confidence in their own professionalism (Osgood 2010b) and to challenge perceptions of their role (McGillivray 2008). For instance, practitioners working with the youngest children reported having had the following comments addressed to them by colleagues and parents:

- 'Why are you working here when you've got a degree?'
- 'You'll just be wasted down there!' 'Why are you bothering to do a degree if you are only working with the babies?
- 'Oh, so will you be working with the older children now?'

A shared learning approach means that the profile of work with babies and toddlers is raised as a natural consequence of being an integral part of practice discussed by the group as a whole. However, this also drew attention to the way that the particular issues of working with babies and toddlers may become subsumed into a generic category of pre-school children. Limited professional development opportunities focusing on the specific needs of this age group were a concern for some as was the tendency for many books purporting to be about 'early years' to ignore children under three. Practitioners working with babies felt this 'invisibility' was a further factor in devaluing their role and reinforced the view that knowledge and experience with older children was sufficient and easily transferable to younger children.

Sharing practice

The growth of a learning community forges professional relationships, which ensure learning continues beyond the timeframe of the EYPS programme. Those who needed to develop their practice and experience with babies and toddlers became increasingly keen to visit settings where they might observe and contribute to high-quality provision, whilst those already working with the younger age group were enthusiastic to demonstrate the rationale for their practice to others who valued their ideas. 'Classroom' relationships thus became working partnerships with potential to maintain the impetus of professional development.

One example illustrates this process in practice as a candidate shared her new initiative to put babies to sleep outside, which she trialled after reading an article highlighting many benefits. Her work colleagues, initially sceptical, were soon won over by the children's increased liveliness and attentiveness whilst awake. In addition, greater resistance to infections was apparent and parents reported that their children slept better at night time. This experience prompted a general discussion about sleeping babies (including reminiscences from older candidates of being put out to sleep in prams!). Another EYP had an alternative perspective on sleeping; at her setting babies can put themselves to bed in low baskets which enable them to decide for themselves when they are tired and want to sleep – and, importantly, when they are ready to get up again. This raises questions of what values inform decisions about children's well-being and reinforced for all practitioners that enabling a baby to sleep is much more than a care routine; it requires deliberate thought and the deep level, higher-order thinking that Moyles (2001) suggests is necessary to operate emotionally at a mindful level. The impact of the learning community was brought home when one of the tutors visited a setting in a different county nine months later and was shown babies sleeping outside. This practice had developed after an EYP had taken the idea back for her staff team to debate and demonstrates how experience in one learning community can then initiate similar professional debate within another.

Change of perspective

In arguing for the importance of a baby practicum with early childhood students, Recchia and Shin (2010) point out how this provides a context for challenging notions about early childhood teaching and learning. We would suggest this is not only relevant to pre-service students but applies equally to practitioners whose experience with the youngest children is limited. Babies and toddlers require a quite different level of interaction and communication and Recchia and Shin (2010) suggest that apparently 'powerless' babies have the potential to make adults feel vulnerable and insecure when their experience and authority is faced with such a challenge. However, the opportunity to step outside what is familiar also prompts professional growth and deeper understanding. One very experienced practitioner, a former teacher who now runs a nursery school, was surprised how much she enjoyed spending time with this new age group and found a new respect for the capabilities of babies:

> It is the same principles that I use with my children here – language and communication, supporting thinking skills.... I learned so much from it I went every week for months! It really opened my eyes to how much more they are capable of than I had realised and I was amazed how long they would stay with an activity they were interested in. (Reflective account)

This professional challenge not only expands practitioners' understanding but encourages them to review their longstanding practice and approach as they realise the primacy of following the children's lead. Another practitioner, following the long extended pathway, admitted:

> It makes you realise how incredibly important observation is – it's all child-initiated activity with that age-group! It made me aware that although I've always *thought* I was listening to the children so often I had my own agenda of what I wanted them to achieve. That sort of approach just won't work with the younger ones so you have to go right back to basics and rethink everything you do. (Group discussion)

Experiences such as these informed group discussions, substantially challenging preconceptions about the abilities of very young children. The realisation that babies are skilful communicators who engage in sustained shared thinking is a powerful antidote to the image of babies as weak and dependent and raises questions about how children's abilities and competence may be underestimated at all levels.

Informing practice; the influence upwards

Many people involved in the field of early years express concerns about the exertion of downward pressure from school. This can often feel like a one-way street as early years practitioners react to expectations of what children should be able to do when they reach primary school. The 'upwards' influence of the principled approach from Birth to Three (SureStart 2003) on the Early Years Foundation Stage (DCSF 2008) has already been noted so, whilst expectations might flow downwards, the upward impact of principles can exert a counterbalance and act as a stimulus for change. At a more local level the change of perspective noted above was discerned to have this same upwards influence on practice. For instance one practitioner, impressed by babies' concentration and high levels of involvement (Laevers 2005) when playing with treasure baskets took those principles back to her work in a pre-school where she revolutionised the practice through a new approach to resources and planning. Another recognised what she could learn from the youngest children in terms of supporting communication and interaction:

> I realised you need a different 'vocabulary' for babies, not just words but visuals and body language as well. All those things we know already but communicating with babies makes it so much more explicit. They can communicate from birth but it's our response to that, finding ways to tap into it that makes the difference. My experience

in the baby room has affected my practice in making me rethink how development informs communication with the other age groups I work with. (Reflective account)

Discussion

The observations discussed here lie outside more systematic impact evaluation currently being undertaken, but the insights they throw up in respect of working with babies and young children give considerable food for thought and should inform future evaluations. Both the Graduate and Undergraduate Practitioner pathways to EYPS enable practitioners to engage in a process of co-constructing knowledge by making and sharing meaning (Appleby 2010) in keeping with EYPs' envisaged role as change agents (CWDC 2010). In this way the process itself acts as a cultural tool in supporting learning (Engeström 1999) and translating learning into agency within grounded practice. This process does not end with the conferral of status. As they go back to their own settings – scattered over a wide geographical area which includes a number of different local authorities with varying systems of training, support and governance in place – EYPs' membership of other 'tangential and over-lapping learning communities' (Lave and Wenger 1991) multiplies the effect. In addition those who already hold the status and act as mentors are also part of these wider learning communities. Cable and Miller (2008) recognise that such empower-ment can '[lead] to change at the individual and societal level' (2008, 173).

Pugh (2010a) has expressed concern that whilst teachers play a key role in curriculum development their current training is not well suited to a multi-agency role and does not encompass the needs and development of children under three. The tendency to dismiss work with babies as offering less challenge and gratification can be particularly noticeable with trained teachers and some are reluctant to complete EYPS because 'we're not interested in babies' (Parsons, personal communication). Teachers in particular may be resistant to a perceived drop in status (Manning-Morton 2006) and often feel their teaching qualification already evidences ability with children without additional experience. However, although teachers may not have a training that prepares them for the integrated approach necessary for babies and toddlers, it does put them in a strong position to recognise the individual learning that takes place. Therefore those who spend time with the younger age group are able to overcome former 'blind spots' as their preconceptions are challenged and they can use such learning to inform future practice. In this way the necessity to engage with babies and toddlers through gaining EYPS 'transforms their sense of themselves as early childhood teachers' (Recchia and Shin 2010, 139).

Conclusion

Childcare outside the home is now an integral part of modern societies and the recent economic downturn has resulted in an increase in demand for places for under-threes (Gaunt 2009). However, Leach asserts that provision for this age group in particular is of 'dismally low quality' (2009, x). Although the nurture of very young children has moved on from its nineteenth-century roots in welfare, as the infant becomes viewed as an educational rather than a health investment, these different traditions stem from contradictory discourses which have implications for policy and practice with the youngest children. Policy now tells us that every child matters from birth but the UK focus on early years as preparation for what comes next can mean that babies are simply cared for until they reach a stage where they might be productively prepared for school. Current emphasis on readiness for school (Tickell 2011) plus targeted provision for two-year-olds to compensate for perceived deficiencies that may impede future educational attainment (Allen 2011), indicates that this perspective is likely to predominate for the foreseeable future. Pugh (2010b) suggests that the requirements of the 2006 Childcare Act to 'narrow the gap' for children from lower socioeconomic groups may have the unintended consequence of skewing an otherwise broad and balanced curriculum. In addition, although the authors make no such suggestion, there could be a danger that settings might conclude, from the evaluation of the GLF (Mathers et al. 2011), that if EYPs appear to make little impact on younger children from birth to 30 months then they are not necessary with this age group.

A value-based early years philosophy that celebrates the competence of children's present rather than what they may become in the future (James and Prout 1997) requires practitioners who are fully 'tuned in' to children. This is particularly necessary with babies and preverbal children who can teach us to listen, communicate and interact in different, more inclusive ways. Therefore there is much to learn from experienced infant practitioners who may often lead the way in observation, listening to the child's voice and creating opportunities for child-initiated discovery and learning. Mathers et al. (2011) suggest that settings should be encouraged to consider whether their graduate leaders are leading practice across the full 0–5 age range and point out the fact that 91% of EYPs work with older children. They suggest that this deployment of staff is a likely explanation for lack of evidence of the impact of graduate practitioners on provision for babies and toddlers and call for more research to establish the most effective ways of raising quality for under-threes through workforce development. Workforce development is also identified as critically important in the Allen Report (2011), the Field Report (2010) and the Tickell Review of the EYFS, which points out that:

> ... without continued investment in the early years workforce the government will struggle to raise attainment, and in particular to narrow the gap between disadvantaged children and their peers. (Tickell 2011, 42)

Urban and Dalli point out how improvement of early years systems is frequently 'hooked to a strategy to further develop the workforce, which is increasingly seen as central to achieving policy intentions' (2008, 131). The British government's recognition of the importance of the workforce is evident in a recent policy document, *Supporting families in the foundation years* (DFE 2011), which pledges continued investment in graduate level training in early education and childcare. In the accompanying ministerial speech outlining the government's policy direction for the early years Sarah Teather emphasised 'the vital role that skilled and knowledgeable professionals and strong leadership play across the foundation years' (Teather 2011) and she has announced a review to ensure a framework of high-standard qualifications. Such a review is part of the 'continued movement towards EYPS as a leadership profession' (Mathers et al. 2011) and is particularly to be welcomed as it has potential to draw attention to the entire 0–5 age range.

It would seem that all the pieces are now in place in terms of policy and frameworks to support high-quality provision for young children. It is now important to ensure that practice matches aspirations and to bridge the gap between rhetoric and reality by investment in the continuing professional development of the workforce. Cable, Goodliff and Miller (2007 cited in Miller 2008) have argued that students and training providers do not have to be passive recipients of workforce reform, but can be active agents with the power to enable early years practitioners to harness their own agency and thus develop a sense of professional identity. Our work with EYPS candidates suggests that raising the profile of working with under-threes benefits not only children themselves but also practitioners whose sense of professionalism and level of self-understanding is expanded by the process of engaging with these very young children. This supports a view of professionalism as 'a *discourse* as much as a *phenomenon*: as something that is constantly under reconstruction' (Urban and Dalli 2008, 132, emphasis in the original). In this way experience with babies and toddlers provides a stimulus for 'the conversational development of informed practical knowledge' (Edwards 1999) which can empower practitioners to engage in the high-level critical reflection necessary to challenge political prescription (Moyles 2001; Osgood 2010a) and too much emphasis on school readiness.

References

Abbott, L., and H. Moylett. 1997. *Working with under-threes: Responding to children's needs*. Buckingham: Open University Press.

Ailwood, J. 2008. Mothers, teachers, maternalism and early childhood education and care: Some historical connections. *Contemporary Issues in Early Childhood* 8, no. 2: 157–65.

Allen, G. 2011. *Early intervention: The next steps*. London: Cabinet Office.

Anning, A., and A. Edwards. 2006. *Promoting children's learning from birth to five: Developing the new early years professional*. 2nd ed. Buckingham: Open University Press.

Appleby, K. 2010. Reflective thinking, reflective practice. In *Reflective practice in the early years*, ed. M. Reed and N. Canning, 7–23. London: Sage Publications.

Appleby, K., and M. Andrews. 2011. Reflective practice is the key to quality improvement. In *Quality improvement and change in the early years*, ed. M. Reed and N. Canning, 57–72. London: Sage Publications.

Baldock, P. 2011. *Developing early childhood services*. Maidenhead: Open University Press, McGraw-Hill.

Baldock, P., D. Fitzgerald, and J. Kay. 2009. *Understanding Early Years Policy*. London: Sage Publications.

Bennett, J. 2003. Starting strong: The persistent division between care and education. *Journal of Early Childhood Research*. 1, no. 1: 21–48.

Bowlby, J. 1953. *Childcare and the growth of love*. Harmondsworth: Penguin.

Cable, C., and L. Miller.. 2008. Looking to the future. In *Professionalisation in the early years*, ed. L. Miller and C. Cable. London: Sage Publications.

Canella, G. 1997. *Deconstructing early childhood education: Social justice and revolution*. New York: Peter Lang Publications.

Chaiklin, S., and J. Lave, eds. 1993. *Understanding practice: Perspectives on activity and context*. Cambridge: Cambridge University Press.

Children's Workforce Development Council (CWDC) 2010. http://www.cwdcouncil.org.uk/eyps (last accessed June 11, 2011).

Cole, M., and Y. Engeström. 1999. A cultural-historical approach to distributed cognition. In *Distributed cognitions: Psychological and educational considerations*, ed. G. Salomon. Cambridge: Cambridge University Press.

Cole, M., Y. Engeström, and O. Vasquez. 1997. *Mind, culture and activity*. Cambridge: Cambridge University Press.

Department for Children, Schools, Families (DCFS). 2008. *The Early Years Foundation Stage*. London: DCSF.

Department for Education (DFE). 2011. *Supporting families in the foundation years*. http://www.education.gov.uk/childrenandyoungpeople/earlylearningandchildcare/early/a00192398/supporting-families-in-the-foundation-years.

Department for Education, Skills (DfES). 2006. *The Childcare Act 2006.* London: HMSO.

Edwards, A. 1999. Research and practice: Is there a dialogue? In *Theory, policy and practice in early childhood services,* ed. H. Penn, 184–99. Buckingham: Open University Press.

Elfer, P., E. Goldschmied, and D. Selleck. 2003. *Key persons in the nursery: Building relationships for quality provision.* London: David Fulton.

Engeström, Y. 1999. Activity theory and individual social transformation. In *Perspectives on activity theory,* ed. Y. Engeström, R. Miettinen, and R.-L. Punamäki. Cambridge: Cambridge University Press.

Field, F. 2010. *The foundation years: Preventing poor children becoming poor adults.* The report of the independent review on poverty and life chances. London: Cabinet Office. http://www.frankfield.co.uk/review-on-poverty-and-life-chances/.

Gaunt, C. 2009. Crunch drives babies into daycare. *Nursery World,* March 12, 2009.

Goldschmied, E., and S. Jackson. 1994. *People under three: Young children in day care.* London: Routledge.

Gopnik, A.N., A. Meltzoff, and P. Kuhl. 1999. *How babies think.* London: Weidenfield & Nicholson.

James, A., and A. Prout, eds. 1997. *Constructing and reconstructing childhood: Contemporary issues in the sociological study of childhood.* Abingdon: Falmer Press.

Laevers, F. 2005. *Deep level learning and the experiential approach in early childhood and primary education.* Leuven: Leuven University Department of Educational Sciences.

Lancaster, Y.P., and V. Broadbent. 2003. *Listening to young children.* Maidenhead: Open University Press/McGraw-Hill Education.

Lave, J., and E. Wenger. 1991. *Situated learning: Legitimate peripheral participation.* Cambridge: Cambridge University Press.

Lea, M.R., and K. Nicoll, eds. 2002. *Distributed learning: Social and cultural approaches to learning.* London: Routledge Falmer.

Leach, P. 2009. *Childcare today: What we know and what we need to know.* Cambridge: Polity Press.

Manning-Morton, J. 2006. The personal is professional: Professionalism and the birth to three practitioner. *Contemporary Issues in Early Childhood* 7, no. 1: 42–52.

Mathers, S., H. Ranns, A. Karemaker, A. Moody, K. Sylva, J. Graham, and I. Siraj-Blatchford. 2011. *Evaluation of the graduate leader fund. Final report.* London: Department for Education. Available from https://www.education.gov.uk/publications/standard/publicationDetail/Page1/DFE-RR144.

McDowall Clark, R. 2011. Working in the spaces: Shared values and localised practice. Keynote speech given at 11th Conference of the European Affective Education Network in Ljubljana, Slovenia, June 26–29.

McDowall Clark, R., and S. Baylis. 2011. 'Go softly…': The reality of leading practice in early years settings. In *Quality improvement and change in the early years,* ed. M. Reed and N. Canning, 140–15. London: Sage Publications.

McGillivray, G. 2008. Nannies, nursery nurses and early years professionals: Constructions of professional identity in the early years workforce in England. *European Early Childhood Research Journal* 16, no. 2: 242–54.

Miller, L. 2008. Developing professionalism within a regulatory professional framework: Challenges and possibilities. *European Early Childhood Research Journal* 16, no. 2: 255–68.

Moss, P. 2006. Structures, understandings and discourses: Possibilities for re-envisioning the early childhood worker. *Contemporary Issues in Early Childhood* 7, no. 1: 30–41.

Moss, P., and H. Penn. 1996. *Transforming nursery education.* London: Paul Chapman.

Moyles, J. 2001. Passion, paradox and professionalism in early years education. *Early years* 21, no. 2: 81–95.

Nutbrown, C., and J. Page. 2009. *Working with babies and children from birth to three.* London: Sage Publications.

Osgood, J. 2010a. Reconstructing professionalism in ECEC: The case for the 'critically reflective emotional professional'. *Early Years* 30, no. 2: 119–33.

Osgood, J. 2010b. Deconstructing 'professionalism' in the nursery. In *Professionalisation, leadership and management in the early years,* ed. L. Miller and C. Cable. London: Sage Publications.

Pascal, C., and T. Bertram. 2009. Listening to young citizens: The struggle to make real a participatory paradigm in research with young children. *European Early Childhood Research Journal* 17, no. 2: 249–62.

Petrie, S., and S. Owen. 2006. *Authentic relationships in group care for infants and toddlers.* London: Jessica Kingsley.

Pugh, G. 1988. *Services for under fives: Developing a co-ordinated approach.* London: National Children's Bureau.

Pugh, G. 2010a. The policy agenda for early childhood services. In *Contemporary issues in the early years*, 5th ed., ed. G. Pugh and B. Duffy, 7–20. London: Sage Publications.

Pugh, G. 2010b. Improving outcomes for young children: Can we narrow the gap? *Early Years* 30, no. 1: 5–14.

Recchia, S.L., and M. Shin. 2010. 'Baby teachers': How pre-service early childhood students transform their conceptions of teaching and learning through an infant practicum. *Early Years* 30, no. 2: 135–45.

Rinaldi, C. 1993. The emergent curriculum and social constructivism. In *The hundred languages of children*, ed. C. Edwards, L. Gandini, and G. Forman. Norwood, NJ: Ablex.

SureStart. 2003. *Birth to three matters: A framework to support children in their earliest years.* London: DfES/SureStart.

Taggart, G. 2011. Don't we care?: The ethics and emotional labour of early years professionalism. *Early years* 31, no. 1: 85–95.

Teather, S. 2011. Written ministerial statement, July 18. http://publications.parliament.uk/.

Tickell. C. 2011. *The early years: Foundations for life, health and learning. An independent review on the Early Years Foundation Stage to Her Majesty's Government.* http://www. education.gov.uk/tickellreview.

Trevarthen, C. 1993. The functions of emotions in early infant communication and development. In *New perspectives on early communicative development*, ed. J. Nadel and L. Camaiori, 48–81. London: Routledge.

Urban, M., and C. Dalli. 2008. Editorial. *European Early Childhood Research Journal* 16, no. 2: 131–3.

Wenger, E. 1998. *Communities of practice: Learning, meaning and identity.* Cambridge: Cambridge University Press.

Woodhead, M. 2009. The 'modern child' in global contexts: Insights from the Young Lives Project. Paper delivered at the Norwegian Centre for Child Research (NOSEB) Conference, Trondheim, Norway, April 29–30.

Index

Related titles from Routledge

Family Factors and the Educational Success of Children

Edited by William Jeynes

Family Factors and the Educational Success of Children addresses a wide range of family variables and a diverse array of family situations in order to understand the dynamics of the multifaceted relationship between family realities and educational outcomes of children. It provides research on building effective partnerships between parents and teaches the importance of parental style, parental involvement as a means of improving family life, the influence of family factors on children of color, and the role of religion in influencing family and educational dynamics.

This book was published as a double special issue of *Marriage and Family Review*.

August 2009: 234 x 156: 420pp
Hb: 978-0-7890-3761-9
Pb: 978-0-7890-3762-6
Hb: £80 / $130 Pb: £22.99 / $45.95

For more information and to order a copy visit
www.routledge.com/9780789037619

Available from all good bookshops

Related titles from Routledge

The Internationalisation of Higher Education

Towards a new research agenda in critical higher education studies

Edited by Eva Hartmann

We are in the middle of a fundamental transformation of the global architecture which is challenging the supremacy of the US, and to a certain extent of Europe, in economic and also in normative terms. The essays in this volume shed light on the role of higher education (HE) and its internationalisation in this transformation, focusing on the different regions of the world. These empirical studies are part of a new research agenda in HE studies, going beyond a 'higher educationism' limiting itself to a simple description of institutional changes in HE in the light of internationalisation. They advance an interdisciplinary perspective drawing on accounts from critical theory, international relations and international political economy. This perspective analyses the strategic selectivity, transformation and struggles related to this major transformation of HE and its contribution to a new global architecture.

This book was originally published as a special issue of *Globalisation, Societies and Education*.

June 2011: 246 x 174: 160pp
Hb: 978-0-415-67227-6
£85 / $145

For more information and to order a copy visit
www.routledge.com/9780415672276

Available from all good bookshops